The In-house Counsel Compliance Companion

Tracey Calvert

Globe Law
and Business

Author
Tracey Calvert

Managing director
Sian O'Neill

The In-house Counsel Compliance Companion
is published by

Globe Law and Business Ltd
3 Mylor Close
Horsell
Woking
Surrey GU21 4DD
United Kingdom
Tel: +44 20 3745 4770
www.globelawandbusiness.com

Printed and bound by CPI Group (UK) Ltd, Croydon CR0 4YY, United Kingdom

The In-house Counsel Compliance Companion

ISBN 9781787424982
EPUB ISBN 9781787424999
Adobe PDF ISBN 9781787425002

DISCLAIMER
This publication is intended as a general guide only. The information and opinions which it contains are not intended to be a comprehensive study, or to provide legal or financial advice, and should not be treated as a substitute for legal advice concerning particular situations. Legal advice should always be sought before taking any action based on the information provided. The publishers bear no responsibility for any errors or omissions contained herein.

Table of contents

Preface

It is lazy to suggest that there are only two types of solicitors and to describe them as either private practitioners or in-house practitioners. The development of legal practice in recent years means that there are opportunities to practise in many different ways.

Private practitioners, for example, can be freelancers, practise from virtual offices, in traditional partnerships and in alternative business structures with non-lawyer owners.

To describe the alternative to private practice with the phrase in-house is equally too simplistic. This is too broad a description for the variety of ways in which solicitors can operate outside of private practice. Here, it is not so much the form of the practice but rather it is the very many different sources of employment opportunities that are available to those who choose the in-house, or employed, solicitor career path.

In-house solicitors, or counsel as they are often described, can be working in local and national government, for public bodies, for regulatory bodies, charities and in commerce and industry. They can work in England and Wales and overseas. The common bond will be the fact that in all these different sources of employment, the solicitor is a person who is admitted to the roll of solicitors and is bound to other solicitors through membership of a common profession with professional status and values. The implication of this position will unfold in different ways largely dependent on the source of the employment, so that a solicitor working in-house for a public authority will face different challenges to those faced by their fellow professionals working in a commercial business.

The intention of this book is to focus on the position of in-house counsel employed in commerce and industry, whether that is for a business which is subject to its own regulatory oversight (such as might be the case in the financial services industry and the pharmaceutical industry) or a business which is wholly profit-making in its objectives.

The challenge for in-house counsel in these settings is to make a professional mark; to identify the regulatory restrictions that apply to them and to accept the ethical behaviours that must be demonstrated notwithstanding the environment in which they provide their services, and also to provide services in accordance with their contract of employment.

Chapter I:

Some introductory thoughts for in-house counsel

Why does the legal profession survive despite all the pressures of twenty-first-century business? Despite all the competition from other legal service providers, the ability of legal service users to access information on the internet, and do-it-yourself lawyering that is possible, why is the solicitor's profession still in existence?

The quick answer comes with an easy-to-understand concept: the majority of consumers continue to have confidence in us and our professionalism. The more detailed answer includes an explanation as to why this is so and with this, it is necessary to consider the constraints that we must observe when we provide services to our clients.

The constraints are imposed on us through regulatory and legal duties we must achieve, and because of the professional ethics which we must display. How we achieve this is through compliance.

Regulation, compliance and ethics are the topics of this book. Some critics of this trio of requirements, including some colleagues in different parts of your business and even, dare it be said out loud, some lawyers with whom you may share office space, will suggest that these concepts are an extra, unnecessary and expensive burden. However, it is the view of the author that without regulation, compliance and ethics it would be harder for solicitors to maintain their competitive edge in this increasingly diverse and competitive marketplace.

There is no lessening of these duties, or watering down of key messages, for in-house lawyers. You make up a sizeable and growing proportion of the solicitor population and you are expected to comply with the same standards, principles and rules as private practitioners. Public interest standard setting, the focus on consumers and services to clients are all topics which have a bearing on how you deliver legal services to your more exclusive client base.

Undoubtedly your client base – your employer and connected parties, and occasionally in the right conditions also members of the public – look to you for well-considered, impartial support motivated by the need to act in their best interests. You are regarded as trustworthy and as trusted advisers. Clients value your training and need your expertise to protect, promote and defend their position. They expect professionalism knowing that for you, this is steeped in well-established ethical concepts. They expect good counsel and counselling from you.

How often do we read descriptions of in-house counsel as the ethical voice of the business? This role, and these expectations, come at a personal cost to the incumbent. At all times, you must be able to demonstrate that nothing or no one will quieten that ethical voice or stamp on your professionalism. Be under no misunderstandings about the need to demonstrate this and know there are consequences if this is not happening.

For the purposes of this book, we are using the term regulation to mean the principles, rules and other requirements that govern our processes and behaviour. Solicitors qualified in England and Wales

"You make up a sizeable and growing proportion of the solicitor population and you are expected to comply with the same standards, principles and rules as private practitioners."

must consider the role of the Solicitors Regulation Authority (SRA) in this context.

The SRA regulates all such solicitors, regardless of where or how they practise. The SRA does this in compliance with the Legal Services Act 2007, and other statutory entitlements, and because it is an approved regulator. It must ensure that its style and policy support what are described as the regulatory objectives in section 1 of the Legal Services Act which are all, directly or indirectly, designed to maintain professionalism and deliver consumer-centric achievements.

Compliance is a responsibility thrust upon individual solicitors. The challenge in your environment is to make others appreciate your regulated traits and to ensure that you are able to display these. In using this term, we mean compliance with the previously mentioned principles, rules, requirements and other similar obligations which have been variously created, described and enforced by the SRA.

Ethics (sometimes also described as professional ethics, legal ethics or professional conduct) describes the entry point standards of behaviour within the profession.

These duties incorporate how we are expected to behave toward our clients, the court, each other and indeed the public at large.

Regulation, compliance and ethics link and overlap. The loss of any one of these components from an individual's way of working makes survival or longevity more difficult to achieve.

This means that the following truths must be acknowledged and evidenced:

- Regulation maintains the standing of the legal profession and we are all answerable to a regulatory body, the SRA.
- Compliance with regulatory standards must be in evidence; we must be able to prove that we are complying with these regulatory requirements.
- Professional ethics must be part of individual decision making.
- That all of the above must reflect current requirements – as imposed variously by the regulator, other external forces and our client base – and with the acceptance that this is a dynamic topic.

And, finally, thinking about regulation, compliance and ethics means that there must be an assessment of risk and how to manage risk. We are describing the risk that we may breach or not comply with our regulatory, compliance and ethical duties. For these purposes risk management denotes the identification of possible risk events and the measures that are implemented to identify and mitigate these risks.

This book is intended to assist busy in-house counsel with essential knowledge about these topics. It is a reference manual for anyone needing to satisfy themselves that they can demonstrate accountability and that their responses to regulation, compliance and ethics will withstand scrutiny. It identifies the key messages that employers and business colleagues must understand about your unique starting point, position and need to satisfy your own regulator that they can have trust in you.

In each chapter, the key topics are discussed with an explanation of essential knowledge and suggestion for practical solutions. The knowledge narrative draws on regulatory expectations, ethical behaviours and various cases and SRA disciplinary findings to demonstrate why particular subjects are relevant and the consequences of misunderstandings. Commentary of disciplinary decisions is drawn from the public records. The practical solutions include compliance strategies, top tips, checklists and tables and contributions from various thought leaders adding their own perspective and experience to the discussions.

Regulation, compliance and ethics matter! It is essential that you understand what is expected of each individual within the profession and have answers to the questions on which you will be tested. Only the correct answers will keep you certificated and able to practise.

Chapter II:

Essential knowledge about the Solicitors Regulation Authority

----

Whatever the type of business in which you are employed, it must never be forgotten that you are first and foremost a solicitor and therefore a member of a regulated community.

This fact has consequences; if you are employed in a business which is not itself part of a regulated industry then you are different, and you find yourself in a distinctive position compared with the non-lawyer colleagues with whom you share office space. The challenge is to ensure that these colleagues recognise that your regulated status means that your starting point is not your employment contract and duties as an employee, but instead is the need to ensure that you do nothing which undermines or compromises your regulated status.

In contrast, if you are employed as in-house counsel within another regulated industry – perhaps financial services or maybe the medical or pharmaceutical industries – you are working with colleagues who understand (or, perhaps more accurately, should understand) the purpose of regulation and the restrictions that this status brings to the business. The business has to comply with its own industry standards and, no doubt, part of your employment as in-house counsel is to support this. Again, the difference between you and your colleagues is that you have two regulatory bodies to please rather than just one.

A brief history of legal services regulation

The regulation of legal services in England and Wales has been subject to fundamental changes since the beginning of this century which might take some lawyers by surprise. It is important to understand how solicitors are regulated as this supports an understanding of what it is necessary to demonstrate to ensure that personal certification to practise law is not compromised.

A brief explanation of recent regulatory developments is necessary. Not because this is a subject which you will want to discuss with work colleagues but because it is essential to understand the purpose of the regulation of lawyers and the recent history which has culminated in the current style of regulation. In other words, knowing the reasons for regulation, and the expectations that vest in regulated individuals, will help with the difficult decisions and conversations that an in-house solicitor must sometimes have with unregulated colleagues, or differently regulated colleagues, and their employer.

To cut a long story short, for a relatively long period of time, solicitors of England and Wales were regulated by the Law Society of England and Wales. The Law Society had many functions; running alongside regulatory duties (which ranged from educational requirements, standards setting, supervision and disciplinary work), it also had a representative role supporting and promoting solicitors and dealt with service complaints from members of the public. This latter function was performed by a branded team (and probably the most infamous of its titles was the Office for the Supervision of Solicitors or OSS), but this was in fact simply a part of the Law Society organisation. Other legal service providers were subject to similar methods of regulatory oversight and representative professional bodies, and the view expressed in some quarters was that legal services regulation was in dire need of an overhaul.

The Clementi Report[1] of 2004 found that the system of regulation in force at that time was not sustainable and did not protect the public interest. The review led to the Legal Services Act 2007 and current regulation of the legal services industry in England and Wales is moulded by this statute.

Key features of modern regulation which have come about as a direct consequence of the Legal Services Act are as follows: the introduction of the Legal Services Board[2] which has an oversight function; regulation of the profession must be independent and separate from representation; regulators must be approved by the Legal Services Board; rules must comply with regulatory objectives described in the Legal Services Act; competition in the legal services market is encouraged with the establishment of alternative business structures enabling lawyers to own and manage legal practices with non-lawyers; service complaints from all sectors of the market are considered by an independent body called the Office for Legal Complaints[3] (also known as the Legal Ombudsman or LeO).

The Solicitors Regulation Authority (SRA)[4] is currently the approved regulator of solicitors of England and Wales. It is also authorised to recognise or license businesses to provide legal services (ie, private practice entities) although this role is less relevant to in-house counsel working outside of private practice. It issues standards, principles and rules which regulated individuals are required to achieve. These are currently described as the SRA Standards and Regulations (the SRA STaRs).[5] The Law Society of England and Wales no longer has a role in

---

1   Legal Services Board, History of legal reforms, https://legalservicesboard.org.uk/about-us/history-of-the-reforms.

2   https://legalservicesboard.org.uk.

3   www.legalombudsman.org.uk.

4   www.sra.org.uk.

5   www.sra.org.uk/solicitors/standards-regulations/.

regulatory work other than as a primary stakeholder. It has retained its role as the representative body for solicitors and will often be seen promoting the interests of its membership with the SRA and in wider circles.[6]

The SRA has been given approved regulator status by the Legal Services Board which has a role to ensure the SRA regulates in the public interest and in accordance with the regulatory objectives described in the Legal Services Act 2007.[7] In doing this, it is answerable to the Legal Services Board. Because of the public interest objectives, and the Legal Services Act, the SRA's remit is very different to that of its predecessor. Noticeably, for in-house counsel, it is important to know that the SRA has to be more interested in this form of practice than was the case with the Law Society.

The regulatory objectives which it must achieve are to protect and promote the public interest; to support the constitutional principle of the rule of law; to improve access to justice; to promote competition in the provision of legal service; to encourage an independent, strong, diverse and effective legal profession; to increase understanding of the citizen's legal rights and duties; and to promote and maintain adherence to what are described as professional principles. These professional principles are the behaviours which are expected of authorised individuals such as independence, integrity, the maintenance of proper standards and confidentiality.

The SRA works in a style described as risk-based regulation. In colloquial terms this simply means that it prioritises its work so that it can focus on risks that are more likely to undermine the regulatory objectives in the Legal Services Act. All solicitors, however they practise, are expected to identify those risks which exist in their environment and take steps to manage and mitigate the impact of risk events. Currently, the SRA regards such topics as lack of diversity in the profession, information and cyber security threats and lack of integrity and ethics as major

---

6   www.lawsociety.org.uk.
7   Legal Services Act 2007, section 1(1).

threats. Identification of these risks informs the SRA's work, and they expect an appropriate response. With diversity, for example, all members of the profession are expected to consider what they do to contribute to the detection and mitigation of its lack; what they can do to develop an inclusive workplace culture, whether there are fair ways to allocate work and to consider whether everyone has the same opportunities in a level playing field environment.[8]

In other words, the SRA's work is less motivated by concerns triggered by client complaints than was the case with its predecessor, although of course it does continue to deal with misconduct allegations brought to its attention in this way. However, it is necessarily more interested in managing the risks which have an impact on its own approved regulator status, on the profession and its collective reputation as being trustworthy advisers and in respect of matters that cause most detriment to the clients and consumers dependent on our services. This is relevant to in-house counsel regardless of who their employer is or what type of legal services they provide. Not only does the Legal Services Board expect to see proportionate regulation of the whole profession, risk-based regulation lends itself to a more obvious need to consider risks present in all types of legal practice.

With this understanding, and acknowledging this change in focus, the SRA is keen to ensure that its attention extends to all solicitors regardless of their type of employment. This has led to a renewed interest in the work of the in-house community and a commitment to consider regulatory risks as posed by in-house work. Whereas in the not-too-distant past, the in-house solicitor was able to enjoy a fairly long-distanced and untroubled relationship with their regulator, the SRA expects more from in-house counsel. This includes having two-way conversations about regulatory and ethical behaviours with the need for the regulated individual to provide reassurances that they understand the standards set by the SRA and provide assurances that they do not pose a regulatory risk.

8   See SRA Risk Outlook, www.sra.org.uk/risk/outlook/risk-outlook-2020-21/.

"Whereas in the not-too-distant past, the in-house solicitor was able to enjoy a fairly long-distanced and untroubled relationship with their regulator, the SRA expects more from in-house counsel."

Practising certificates

One of the roles of the approved regulator is to authorise individuals to provide legal services. The SRA has the power to not only issue practising certificates, thereby entitling the certificate-holder to practise as a solicitor, but it also has powers to remove the same and/or impose conditions on practising rights. Its role in this area supports the regulatory objectives described in the Legal Services Act, as certification will be removed if this is deemed to be in the public interest.

For many in-house counsel, the relationship with the SRA is focused on this topic and practising certificate conversations.

It is a deeply rooted, but mostly incorrect myth, that in-house counsel do not require practising certificates. Sometimes this belief is based on the assumption that a practising certificate is not necessary simply because the individual does not work in private practice or does not provide legal services to members of the public, or perhaps because they describe themselves as counsel rather than as solicitors or lawyers. These myths need to be quashed once and for all.

To be clear, the circumstances in which an individual who is on the roll of solicitors can provide legal services without holding a current practising certificate are rare. Anyone who does practise uncertificated, without being entitled to rely on one of the very limited statutory exceptions that exist, is likely to find that they have committed an offence under the Solicitors Act 1974 and also are in breach of their regulatory duties.[9]

The practising certificate myth-busting questions include the following:

1. **Can in-house counsel rely on a statutory carve-out (or statutory exemption) to practise without a practising certificate?**
    Section 88 of the Solicitors Act 1974 provides an exemption from having a practising certificate limited to the principal solicitor (and any solicitor who is a clerk or officer appointed to act for that

---

9   See SRA Authorisation of Individual Regulations, www.sra.org.uk/solicitors/standards-regulations/authorisation-individuals-regulations/.

solicitor) to the Treasury, the Church Commissioners, the Duchy of Cornwall and any other public department. In practice, this statutory exemption does not apply to many types of employed lawyers. The SRA does not provide assistance or give safe harbour-type guidance on the application of this exemption. The judgement as to whether this exemption benefits an individual is left with that individual who might be asked by the SRA to justify their decision.

2. **Can an individual avoid a practising certificate if they do not hold themselves out as a solicitor and do not undertake reserved legal activities?**

   Reserved legal activities are legal services which only certain qualified persons can perform.[10] A solicitor with a current practising certificate is a qualified person. Therefore, regardless of job description or any other factor, a solicitor must have a current certificate in force to be able to provide these services. The individual's job title is largely not relevant in these circumstances. The categories of reserved legal activities are defined by statute and are listed in Table 1.

3. **If an individual is employed, or otherwise described, as counsel, and not solicitor, do they need a practising certificate?**

   The solicitor title is protected by law so that unqualified persons are committing an offence if they use this. The counsel description is not similarly protected but it is a term which is used to mean a lawyer, in particular a lawyer in an in-house or international role. This connects its use with the term lawyer as used in the SRA STaRs Glossary to denote a member of the following professions:

   - The profession of solicitor, barrister or advocate of the UK.
   - An authorised person other than one authorised by the SRA.
   - Any profession approved by the SRA for registered foreign lawyer status.

---

10   Legal Services Act 2007, section 12.

- Any other regulated legal profession specified by the SRA for the purpose of this definition.

Drilling down, the SRA says that the phrase 'lawyer of England and Wales' means a solicitor or otherwise an individual authorised to carry on legal activities in England and Wales but excludes an individual registered with the Bar Standards Board under the European Communities (Lawyer's Practice) Regulations 2000.

In other words, as the term counsel denotes a lawyer, and in turn lawyer means someone who is a regulated professional, solicitors described as counsel must have a practising certificate.

Table 1: Reserved legal services

Reserved legal services	What is included in reservation?
The exercise of any rights of audience	• The right to appear before a court
The conduct of litigation	• Issuing proceedings before any court in England and Wales • Commencing, prosecuting or defending proceedings • Ancillary functions related to the proceedings
Reserved instrument activities	• Preparing any instrument or charge, making an application or lodging a document for registration under the Land Registration Act 2002 • Preparing any other instrument connected with real or personal estate or any instrument relating to court proceedings in England and Wales
Probate activities	• Preparing probate papers for the purposes of the law of England and Wales or in respect of any proceedings in this jurisdiction
Notarial activities	• Activities performed by notaries under the Public Notaries Act 1801
Administration of oaths	• Exercising the powers of a commissioner for oaths

4. **If an employer will not pay for a practising certificate, can an individual practise uncertificated?**

   No. Meeting the expense of the annual practising certificate is an individual responsibility. While it is customary for this expense to be met by the employer, this will be an employment term. In circumstances in which a practising certificate is required and the employer does not meet that expense, this is not a legitimate reason to practise uncertificated.

5. **If an individual is a *locum*, or has a temporary contract, do they need a practising certificate?**

   Yes. Temporary employment of any type does not override the legal and regulatory duties as found in the Solicitors Act 1974 and the SRA Authorisation of Individuals Regulations.

Applying for a practising certificate

Application is made to the SRA during the annual renewal process which takes place in October of each year and by a submission to the SRA's portal system 'mySRA'.[11] This can be done individually or through a block renewal procedure whereby a number of applications can be made by one individual, such as might be expedient in an in-house legal team.

A fee is payable by individuals which comprises the regulatory fee and a contribution towards the SRA Compensation Fund (the latter being payable by all practising solicitors except individuals employed as Crown Prosecutors). Reduced fees are available to deal with such events as maternity leave and furloughing.

Competency

The practising certificate application contains a number of questions which must be answered by the applicant, including one that relates to an individual's continuing professional development. This is described as continuing competency, and the applicant is asked to confirm that

11   www.sra.org.uk/mysra/.

they have reflected on their practice and identified any learning and development needs.

Again, this is language connected with the modern style of regulation. The SRA describes competency as "being the ability to perform the roles and tasks required by one's job to the expected standard".[12]

To be clear, competency is so much more than simply keeping up to date with legal knowledge although, it goes without saying, that this is part of what is expected from a certificated individual. The mandatory duties about competency are set out in the SRA Code of Conduct for Solicitors, Registered European Lawyers and Registered Foreign Lawyers so that in Chapter 3 we are informed that:

> *3.2 You ensure that the service you provide to clients is competent and delivered in a timely manner.*
>
> *3.3 You maintain your competence to carry out your role and keep your professional knowledge and skills up to date.*[13]

Regulatory assistance is provided in the SRA's Statement of Solicitor Competence[14] which describes the behaviours which solicitors should be able to demonstrate. These are broken down into four areas as follows:

- Section A – Ethics, professionalism and judgement;
- Section B – Technical legal practice;
- Section C – Working with other people; and
- Section D – Managing themselves and their own work.

In total there are about 90 different behaviours that are indicative of a solicitor's competence. The expectation is that these will be applied to the circumstances and experience of the individual so that, for example, the way in which a senior member of an in-house legal team

---

12   www.sra.org.uk/solicitors/resources/cpd/competence-statement/.
13   SRA Code of Conduct for Solicitors, RELs and RFLs, chapter 3, paragraphs 3.2 and 3.3.
14   www.sra.org.uk/solicitors/resources/cpd/competence-statement/.

demonstrates competency will be different to the way in which a newly qualified individual would comply.

The behaviours could trigger a number of learning and development conversations. In-house counsel are likely to need external resources for help in keeping up to date with expected ethical standards and technical legal practice. Less experienced lawyers might also gain competency skills through shadowing and working with more experienced colleagues plus personal study such as, for example, reading a book like this. However, resources designed to support all staff within the business can be used by solicitors to establish their competency for regulatory purposes so that courses on soft skills such as coaching and communications are beneficial; equality and diversity training helps, as does acquiring knowledge about the business because this will support the requirement to tailor legal services to the needs of the client.

Top tips for ensuring a good working relationship with the SRA

✔ Ensure that the SRA has current practising details – these must be included in the public register.

✔ Keep your 'mySRA' details up to date.

✔ If your practising certificate application is made as part of a bulk renewal exercise then be confident that this is being handled properly.

✔ Keep learning and development records so that competency attainments are evidenced.

✔ If in a position of responsibility within the legal team, ensure that colleagues are also doing all of the above. In addition – and bearing in mind the risks of unqualified persons using certain titles – be confident that no one might be in a position where they are inadvertently holding themselves out as a solicitor or a legally qualified person. Solicitors and lawyers of other jurisdictions (eg, Australian solicitors etc) must ensure that no one is misled into thinking that they are a solicitor of England and Wales.

Chapter III:

Essential ethical knowledge for in-house counsel

Ethical behaviour is the defining characteristic of professionals. It is a set of values which exemplify what it means to be a particular type of professional person. Meeting ethical standards is a bench marker, and much of the work undertaken by the regulatory body is to test its professional membership against these defining characteristics when appropriate.

This position is based on a number of suppositions, first and foremost that we will know ethical behaviour when we see it and that we will be able to demonstrate an ethical response. Sadly, the teaching of ethics is frequently a little hit and miss, with many teaching and testing requirements dictating that ethics is taught and tested pervasively, so that building up ethical knowledge is made much harder. Instead, developing an appropriate level of ethical awareness is often a matter of luck based on a combination of factors such as the environment in which you work, the willingness for there to be a culture of compliance and, to be frank, the knowledge of colleagues about this important topic and their ability to influence others.

THOUGHT LEADERSHIP

Being ethically aware is vital. The following contribution is from **Francisco Esparraga***, an author and senior lecturer at the School of Law at the University of Notre Dame, in Australia.*

Ethical thinking should pervade all aspects of any professional practice. Whether it is providing legal advice about a contract for the sale of land; financial advice with regards to investment options; medical advice regarding treatment choices; or in-house government public servant advice to Ministers, it should not matter. Obedience to a comprehensive code of ethics is a defining characteristic of every professional person.

It is important to note that there is no magic procedure which can guarantee that every professional will always attain the required ethical standard. It is about a process which professionals need to continually strengthen when turning their minds to and take steps to ensure that they fulfil their professional obligations. This process will always be weakened if professionals turn a blind eye to and ignore inappropriate unethical behaviour.

What is certain is that professionals will not be successful in adapting if they reject the ethical duties which lie at the heart of being professional.

Historically, the personal need for knowledge, our society's need for skilled administrators, for technically trained experts and service personnel with a variety of skills, saw the emergence in our society of more clearly defined occupational groups called professions.

The major growth of the professions occurred with the large-scale industrial revolution which followed the application of scientific discoveries. The growth of industry brought with it the complex division of labour associated with it. It also destroyed the guilds as the skills of artisans were replaced by machine production, but the personal service offered by lawyers could not be so easily removed. At the same time, the growth of scientific knowledge also affected the character of the education and the training provided by the universities, but the hallmarks of professionalism were already in place: mastery or status within society; being organised into a body by occupation; requiring prolonged and specialised training and education; offering autonomy within job roles; having collective influence within society and being self-regulatory.

No single definition of a profession attracts global acceptance. The traits, characteristics and attributes of professions have always been in flux. The variety of definitions serves to highlight the difficulty. The earliest instance of the use of the word 'profession' in the English-speaking world was in the *Oxford English Dictionary* dating from 1541.

At the risk of being too simplistic, debate over the context of any definition of profession turns on whether the creation of the profession is primarily a matter of politics or sociology. Professionalism lies on a continuous scale and the position which any vocation occupies on that scale will depend on the particular values that may be ascribed to certain general properties which are seen to be characteristic of that profession.

Morris Cogan, in 'The Problem of Defining a Profession' (1955),[1] defined a profession as:

A vocation whose practice is founded upon an understanding of the theoretical structure of some department of learning or science, and upon the abilities accompanying such

---

[1] M Cogan, "The Problem of Defining a Profession" (1955), 297 *Annals of the American Academy of Political Science* 107.

understanding. This understanding and these abilities are applied to the vital practical affairs of man. The practices of the profession are modified by knowledge of a generalized nature and by the accumulated wisdom and experience of mankind, which serve to correct the errors of specialism. The profession, serving the vital needs of man, considers its first ethical imperative to be altruistic service to the client.

This definition is notable for the notion of 'altruistic service to the client' as a distinguishing feature of the professions and this has been echoed by many other writers.

There is also the view that the existence of a professional association is an essential feature of a profession. While any occupational group can form an association, it is not so much the mere existence of the association which is important, but the nature of the values which the association fosters or supports. In particular, the requirement that members of the association should adhere to rules of conduct, backed by sanctions.

While there is continuing disagreement as to the relative importance of the characteristics of the professions, the main characteristics about which there is considerable agreement seem to be:

- a high level of generalised and systematic knowledge leading to a formal qualification;
- work directed towards general community or cultural benefit rather than to individual self-interest;
- a large measure of autonomy correlated with recognition of responsibility towards clients or employers, and the public;
- self-consciousness and a measure of corporate control of professional group through lengthy socialisation processes and traditional codes of conduct;

- money and honours regarded as symbols of work achievement and thus as ends in themselves rather than as means to serve other self-interests.[2]

While definitions have emphasised the significance of employing an attitude of responsibility, in more recent times, the emphasis on ethics in the definition of profession can be seen in the definition adopted by Professions Australia:

A profession is a disciplined group of individuals who adhere to ethical standards and hold themselves out as, and are accepted by the public as possessing special knowledge and skills in a widely recognized body of learning derived from research, education and training at a high level, and who are prepared to apply this knowledge and exercise these skills in the interests of others.

It is inherent in the definition of a profession that a code of ethics governs the activities of each profession. Such codes require behaviour and practice beyond the personal moral obligations of an individual. They define and demand high standards of behaviour in respect to the services provided to the public and in dealing with professional colleagues. Further, these codes are enforced by the profession and are acknowledged and accepted by the community.[3]

In the words of United States Supreme Court Justice Sandra Day O'Connor:

---

2   See, Francisco Esparraga, *Ethical Legal Practice and Professional Conduct*, LexisNexis Butterworths Australia, 2019 at 10, citing B Barber, 'Is American Business Becoming Professionalized?' in E A Tiryakian (ed) *Sociological Theory, Values and Sociocultural Change*, Free Press, London, 1963.

3   Professions Australia, *About Professions Australia, Definition of a Profession*, 1997, adopted at the Annual General Meeting, 26 May 1997.

> *One distinguishing feature of any profession, unlike other occupations that may be equally respectable, is that membership entails an ethical obligation to temper one's selfish pursuit of economic success by adhering to standards of conduct that could not be enforced either by legal fiat or through the discipline of the market.*[4]

In short, 'professionalism' is a certain something that a professional will exude, and which is expected by those dealing with them. At the very heart of professionalism will be ethics.

It is also important to acknowledge that the concept of professions is a developing one which will never remain static. History has demonstrated how the development of new areas of knowledge has opened up the possibilities for professions far beyond the 'learned' trinity of professions.

In a world where knowledge is expanding boundaries almost every day and such knowledge is accessible to larger numbers of people, and where complexity and specialised expertise is necessary, more and more occupations will enter the realm of the professions. Much more could be said about the question of defining a profession, but it would not be essential to the purpose of this book. It is sufficient to make the following four points:

- The professions have a history as corporate bodies stretching back to the Middle Ages.
- The basis of professional association has been the exercise of a special skill whose benefits are sought by others.
- The foundation and extension of the skills peculiar to the professions have been strongly affected by the emergence of the scientific movement and university training.

4 *Shapero v Kentucky Bar Association* (1988) 486 US 466 at 488.

- The education and training for, and exercise of, specialised skills have important moral consequences for the professional and for the relations between professionals and others.[5]

At the core of the attributes of a professional person is the need for membership of a regulated community and a clear, unequivocal demonstration of ethical behaviour.

The SRA's interest in our ethical behaviours

For a number of reasons, interest in ethics had until very recently centred on the demonstration of ethical behaviour in private practice. Traditionally and previously, the regulator's enforcement agenda was focused more on dealing with complaints about misconduct (ie, unethical behaviour) and these were almost exclusively brought to its attention by disgruntled clients. The codification of ethical behaviours was largely drafted with private practice in mind for many years. The assumption was that ethical behaviour in the in-house practice arena could be justifiably treated differently – dare we say it, sidelined – to private practice.

Of course, this had to change. With the Legal Services Act 2007, we now have an approved regulator (the SRA) needing to prove that its regulatory reach extends to the entire solicitor population. It has to apply risk-based regulation so that the statutorily defined regulatory objectives and professional principles are enforced, and action taken, whenever and wherever there is a threat to this agenda and a threat to the profession's collective reputation.

What we have seen since 2007 is a concerted effort on the part of the SRA to ensure that its ambit extends to the whole solicitors' profession. Ethical behaviours are described in the SRA Standards and Regulations

---

5   Francisco Esparraga, *Ethical Legal Practice and Professional Conduct,* LexisNexis Butterworths Australia, 2019 at 16.

"Ethical behaviours are described in the SRA Standards and Regulations ('the STaRs') and in-house counsel are required to know which parts apply to them and develop ways to demonstrate compliance in practice."

('the STaRs') and in-house counsel are required to know which parts apply to them and develop ways to demonstrate compliance in practice.

This is not without challenges. Because of the previous and more tenuous relationship between in-house lawyers and their regulator, it remains the position that many in this position do not consider ethical behaviours in the same way as private practitioners. Ethics, or standards, must always be considered before anything else. Those in private practice might find it easier to consider and prioritise their own ethical behaviour before the interests of their clients simply because their clients are not also their employers and work colleagues, and the distance makes ethical decision making somehow less complicated. The dynamic between in-house counsel and the client (which triggers a number of the ethical duties) is necessarily less detached, usually more long-lasting and definitely fuzzier because of the employment contract which connects the two sides. Private practitioners operate in an environment where the need to maintain authorised status motivates everyone to behave in an ethical way, whereas in-house counsel have the pressure of exerting their own ethical behaviours in a business which is not necessarily interested in the SRA.

Chapter IV:

Sources of ethical knowledge for in-house counsel (1)

An introduction to the SRA Standards and Regulations – the SRA Principles

A solicitor who does not have any knowledge of the STaRs is in a precarious position. This knowledge is assumed by the SRA which is entitled to put a regulated individual to the test. This is because the STaRs are described as "the standards and regulations we expect our regulated community to achieve and observe, for the benefit of the clients they serve and in the public interest".[1]

The STaRs were launched in November 2019, replacing the first version of the SRA regulatory rulebook which had been known as the SRA Handbook. The SRA's expectation is that individual solicitors will know this fact, and also be able to identify those parts of the STaRs

---

1 www.sra.org.uk/solicitors/standards-regulations/.

which are relevant to them because of their circumstances and be able to demonstrate compliance in practice.

The parts of the STaRs which focus on a solicitor's ethical duties and professional behaviours are the SRA Principles and the SRA Code of Conduct for Solicitors, Registered European Lawyers and Registered Foreign Lawyers. Other parts of the STaRs might be relevant because of what you do or may have no relevance at all because you are employed as in-house counsel rather than working in private practice.

It goes without saying that the STaRs are littered with references to clients. This has a defined meaning; it is the "person for whom you act and, where the context permits, includes prospective and former clients".[2] Applied to in-house practice, this will usually refer to your employer, although where the conditions permit, this can also be someone else to whom legal services are provided. Acting for clients who are not the employer, and the specific ethical considerations which must be considered are described in Chapter V. Ignoring references to clients can sometimes mean that ethical considerations are missed, and it makes sense to refer to all individuals and entities for whom you provide legal services as clients so that the significance is not lost in translation.

SRA Principles

This is essential knowledge for all solicitors regardless of how they practise because, to use the SRA's language: "The SRA Principles comprise the fundamental tenets of ethical behaviour that we expect all those that we regulate to uphold."[3] In other words, understanding the expectations about how we will behave by reference to the language of the Principles is essential. Being able to demonstrate that these behaviours are put into practice is necessary if an individual is going to provide the SRA with the assurances it needs that it is appropriate to have and maintain confidence in them to uphold the collective professional reputation.

---

2 www.sra.org.uk/solicitors/standards-regulations/glossary/.
3 www.sra.org.uk/solicitors/standards-regulations/principles/.

The good news story about the Principles is that we are required to uphold seven behaviours only. Also, the Principles do not contain any surprises for anyone who has reflected on what it means to be a member of the legal profession. The Principles are not particularly original or innovative so there is comfort in this familiarity. We have always recognised core values or basic behaviours and the Principles is simply the latest iteration. The sting in the tail, however, is that the SRA expects to see these behaviours demonstrated not only during our working lives but also in our personal lives and its regulatory reach extends to taking enforcement action against individuals if personal, non-work-related behaviour suggests a breach of a Principle.

The Principles are as follows:

"Principle 1 – you act in a way that upholds the constitutional principle of the rule of law, and the proper administration of justice"

As officers of the court, solicitors should understand the need to not only uphold the rule of law but also to acknowledge that duties to the court will take precedence over other duties in the event of a conflict.

With this knowledge, an immediate workplace tension springs to mind, namely the position any solicitor might find themselves in if their duty to uphold Principle 1 disappoints their client or is contrary to the client's instructions. A private practitioner might find it easier to challenge their client's inappropriate instructions. Working in-house, and for a client who is also the paymaster, might make this a more challenging conversation (hence the justification for earlier observations about the sense of using the solicitor-client language).

Regardless of any discomfort, it is a necessary conversation and a message that must be understood by the client. The conflict between duties to the court and duties to carry out a client's instructions (or, put another way, seemingly a duty to act in a client's best interests) must always be decided in favour of the courts. Neither the judicial system, nor the SRA, will accept any explanation for why this is not the case.

"The SRA expects to see these behaviours demonstrated not only during our working lives but also in our personal lives and its regulatory reach extends to taking enforcement action against individuals."

In the case of *Arthur J S Hall v Simons* [2002] 1 AC 615, Lord Hoffman made the argument for the judicial system:

Lawyers conducting litigation owe a divided loyalty. They have a duty to their clients, but they may not win by whatever means. They also owe a duty to the court and the administration of justice ... Sometimes the performance of these duties to the court may annoy the client. So, it was said, the possibility of a claim for negligence might inhibit the lawyer from acting in accordance with his overriding duty to the court. That would be prejudicial to the interests of justice.

The SRA adds strength to this position by stating in the preamble to the Principles[4] that should there be a conflict:

... those which safeguard the wider public interest (such as the rule of law, and public confidence in a trustworthy solicitors' profession and a safe and effective market for regulated legal services) take precedence over an individual client's interests. You should, where relevant, inform your client of the circumstances in which your duty to the Court and other professional obligations will outweigh your duty to them.

In fact, the SRA is so anxious that we will mismanage this conflict, and thereby fail to uphold Principle 1, that copious amounts of guidance have been published to support understanding.[5] If we act in litigation, we will be expected to be aware of this guidance and if enforcement action is deemed necessary, then we might be asked to explain why we did not take notice of these and similar resources.

In practice, we are told that we are likely to be in breach of Principle 1 if we interfere with and/or abuse the judicial process; if we mislead the court or knowingly or recklessly allow the court to be misled by others; if

---

4 www.sra.org.uk/solicitors/standards-regulations/principles/.

5 SRA paper, *Balancing Duties in Litigation*, November 2018, www.sra.org.uk/globalassets/documents/solicitors/freedom-in-practice/balancing-duties-in-litigation.pdf?version=49922b; SRA Topic guide, 'A guide to the application of Principle 1', www.sra.org.uk/sra/corporate-strategy/sra-enforcement-strategy/enforcement-practice/guide-application-principle-1/.

we fail to comply with powers lawfully exercised by the court or by other enforcement authorities and similar.[6]

For in-house counsel undertaking litigation on behalf of their client, the following are essential sense-testing questions:

- Is the client (employer) aware of my ethical boundaries?
- Am I confident that my own ethical duties are not eroded by my client's instructions?
- Can I raise concerns with senior colleagues in the business if I am being asked to act unethically?
- If I lead a team, or otherwise am in a position of influence in a legal team, do I monitor the compliance of others with this Principle and can I lend support, perhaps in assisting with challenging solicitor-client conversations?
- Do colleagues need training?
- Does my/our understanding of this Principle need to be documented in a compliance manual or similar?

Principle 1's reach extends to the private lives of in-house counsel and all other solicitors. The SRA is clear that Principle 1 might be breached by conduct outside of the workplace which results in a criminal conviction, charge or caution, and in connection with any behaviour that shows a disregard for the concept of the rule of law and its application to everyone in society. It expects to be notified of such matters in a timely fashion, and delay in bringing such matters to its attention is often described as an aggravating factor when enforcement action is being considered.[7] Consider the following examples of behaviours that have faced disciplinary scrutiny that have arisen in connection with Principle 1:

---

6 See SRA Code of Conduct for Solicitors, RELs and RFLs, www.sra.org.uk/solicitors/standards-regulations/code-conduct-solicitors/.

7 SRA Topic guide, 'Criminal offences outside of practice', www.sra.org.uk/sra/corporate-strategy/sra-enforcement-strategy/enforcement-practice/criminal-offences-outside-practice/.

- A solicitor was struck off the roll of solicitors in 2018 for evading £650 in train fares.[8]
- A solicitor was fined £1,000 in 2020 for failing to report a drink-driving conviction promptly to the SRA.[9]
- *SRA v Main* – an in-house solicitor had been convicted of sexual assault offences and racially aggravated assault in a magistrates court. The SRA subsequently brought disciplinary proceedings against him and in respect of various public interest-based examples of non-compliance with the relevant Principles. The Solicitors Disciplinary Tribunal (SDT) imposed a two-year suspension from practice order on him but decided that this would be for a one-year period because Mr Main had not worked for a year prior to the SDT hearing. The SRA appealed this ruling saying that the sanction was too lenient. The High Court agreed with the SRA and ordered that the suspension should be for two years from the date of the SDT hearing.[10]

"Principle 2 – you act in a way that upholds public trust and confidence in the solicitors' profession and in legal services provided by authorised persons"

Although some more experienced lawyers will be more comfortable with language such as not bringing the profession into disrepute rather than this modern form, this is a familiar duty.

If we are to provide competent legal services, it is essential that we behave in a way that upholds trust and confidence. In the landmark regulatory case of *Bolton v Law Society*[11] the benchmark was set with the bold statement that it is essential that solicitors can be "trusted to the ends of the earth".

---

8   SDT case 526759 re Adam Kemeny, 1 November 2018.
9   SDT case 039571 re Oliver Godwin, 21 August 2020.
10   *SRA v Main* [2018] EWHC 3666 (Admin).
11   *Bolton v Law Society* [1993] EWCA Civ 32.

We must establish and maintain a reputation for being trustworthy individuals and therefore trusted advisers. In the in-house context, this Principle must be considered both in the context of the services we provide to our client but also in respect of the way we behave toward third parties when representing our clients.

This latter point triggered SRA action in the form of a regulatory warning notice that was issued in 2014. Regulatory warning notices are used by the SRA to highlight its concerns about specific, normally topical, issues. In this case, the SRA issued a warning notice and addressed it to in-house practitioners to remind them of their obligations when their employers pursued customers of the business for unpaid debts. The solicitors were reminded of their personal duties not to take unfair advantage of the customer's lack of legal knowledge and/or lack of legal advice. This warning notice was prompted after the now defunct payday lender Wonga had admitted using fake law firm names to send legal letters to customers who had fallen behind in their repayments.[12]

In the workplace, the duty of upholding trust and confidence will be met if there is awareness of the need to act in a way that upholds the values of the profession and the attributes of a professional person.

Again, sense-testing questions can be used to evaluate compliance:

- Am I confident that I am regarded as a professional individual?
- In my behaviour toward, and services for, clients, am I confident that I am regarded as a trustworthy member of a profession?
- Does anything about my client's expectations or instructions undermine my professional status?
- Am I prepared to challenge inappropriate behaviour in myself or that I see in others?
- If I am in a senior role, am I able to develop a culture that supports professionalism?

---

12   The Law Society Gazette, "SRA warns lawyers not to mislead third parties", 9 July 2014, www.lawgazette.co.uk/news/sra-warns-in-house-lawyers-not-to-mislead-third-parties/ 5042097.article.

- If I am not in a senior role, am I able to secure support if I feel my professional position is being compromised?
- Is the requirement to notify the SRA of any criminal convictions, charges or cautions understood?

Outside of practice, and/or in the twilight world between work and home, Principle 2 is applied in a way that means behaviours which undermine the profession's collective reputation for trustworthiness are scrutinised. There are two particular areas of concern which the SRA is currently seeking to address: misuse of social media and sexual (and similar) harassment.

The SRA has issued guidance and a warning notice on the use of social media and offensive communications and is emphatic that it will treat seriously any communication sent in a work environment or when acting in a personal capacity and in circumstances where the sender is identifiable.[13] The purpose of warning notices must be noted: they are mostly used to highlight emerging risks, or risks where it is imperative that there are no misunderstandings about the regulatory response, and they are prefaced with a declaration that the SRA may have regard to the warning notice when exercising regulatory functions.

What is clear is that the SRA has concerns about inappropriate communications largely, but not exclusively relating to emails and social media, and that there is the expectation that these will not have "derogatory, harassing, hurtful, puerile, plainly inappropriate" content.[14] Regulatory action will be considered even if no one has read or been affected by the communication. In a guidance note issued to assist with compliance with equality values, the SRA's language is unequivocal and

---

13 SRA Topic guide, 'Use of social media and offensive communications', www.sra.org.uk/sra/corporate-strategy/sra-enforcement-strategy/enforcement-practice/social-media-offensive-communications/; SRA Warning notice, 'Offensive communications', www.sra.org.uk/solicitors/guidance/offensive-communications/.
14 SRA Warning notice, 'Offensive communications', www.sra.org.uk/solicitors/guidance/offensive-communications/.

seeks to confirm that the sentiments from the *Bolton v Law Society* case of 1993 are no less relevant today. Addressing regulated individuals, the SRA says:

> *You are responsible for upholding the reputation of the profession in your professional and personal life and for treating people fairly and with dignity and respect. You are responsible for making sure your personal views are not imposed on and do not have a negative impact on others. This includes expressing extreme personal, moral or political opinions on social media platforms.*[15]

This is not an empty threat. The following are examples of disciplinary action:

- A solicitor was fined £10,000 by the SDT in 2020 after sending a series of abusive Facebook messages to someone he had briefly dated.[16]
- A solicitor was rebuked and fined £1,500 under the terms of a regulatory settlement agreement reached with the SRA in 2019 for posting information on social media when he attended police stations, prisons or courts, often adding where he was and the criminal charges he was advising on and adding inappropriate comments or emoji icons described as "inappropriate and puerile" in the details of the regulatory decision.[17]

It is clear that the bar is raised high, and we are expected to consider the consequences of our social media output.

Similarly, behaviours in and outside the workplace are likely to attract regulatory attention where there is unfair discrimination and sexual harassment. Another topic where regulatory warning notices have

---

15   SRA Guidance, 'The SRA's approach to equality, diversity and inclusion', www.sra.org.uk/solicitors/guidance/sra-approach-equality-diversity-inclusion/.
16   SDT case 481761 re James Andrew Wilson (formerly known as Victor Kruchinkin), June 2020.
17   SRA Regulatory Settlement Agreement re H S Paul, dated 13 August 2019.

been used is with non-disclosure agreements (NDAs),[18] and solicitors are expected to resist using these, or assisting clients in the preparation of these, in circumstances where the intention is to stifle investigations, claims and/or recourse to legal remedies.

In private practice, law firm owners are likely to be criticised where there is a cover-up of serious misconduct of this nature, or it is not reported promptly to the SRA. With in-house practice, the SRA has no regulatory reach over anyone other than regulated solicitors but will look to them not to use NDAs in a way that undermines trust and confidence. As with so many matters, this means it is important that any expectations are managed so that a client understands when you would have to refuse to act on their instructions, such as in drafting an NDA designed to cover up the behaviour of an employee.

Questions to make a self-assessment of an appropriate response include:

- Is there anything about my work, and my client's expectations, that might compromise my ability to uphold Principle 2?
- Particularly, in the area of employment advice, do I understand regulatory requirements about the use of non-disclosure agreements?
- Am I confident that nothing about my social media use is likely to offend regulatory principles?
- Do I caution myself against ill-advised correspondence with colleagues which might bring my trustworthiness into question?
- In senior roles, am I able to influence the behaviours of colleagues so that they understand how Principle 2 pervades their personal lives and they take action to behave appropriately?

18　SRA Warning notice, 'Use of non-disclosure agreements (NDAs)', www.sra.org.uk/solicitors/guidance/non-disclosure-agreements-ndas/.

"Principle 3 – you act with independence"

A solicitor is independent of his client and having regard to his wider responsibilities and the need to maintain the Profession's reputation, [they] must and should on occasion be prepared to say to [their] client "What you seek to do may be legal but I am not prepared to help you do it".[19]

The principle of independence is perhaps the most obviously challenging principle to achieve for in-house counsel who need to be able to say no, when necessary, to a client who is also their employer.

We have already seen how this could become an issue with the examples given about the use of the court and Principle 1, and the use of non-disclosure agreements with Principle 2. In-house counsel is in a different position to many of their fellow employees. While all colleagues have their own moral compass to set, the solicitor has a duty to observe independence of decision making that is based in legal ethics and monitored by its own regulatory body.

Other sources of tension, and forces that can potentially compromise an individual's independence of thought and action can come from third parties or from other colleagues. Nothing or no one should be allowed to come between in-house counsel and their ability to act legally and also ethically.

In-house counsel should ask themselves the following questions:

- Am I confident that I am truly exercising independence of thought when providing services to my client?
- Do I know who to raise concerns with if I am unable to act with independence?
- In a senior role, am I able to lead by example by acting in an unfettered and uninfluenced way when providing legal services?

---

19 In the matter of Paul Francis Simms, SDT 2002, as quoted in the SRA Guidance 'Walking the line', www.sra.org.uk/risk/risk-resources/balancing-duties-litigation/.

- In a junior role, do I have someone I can speak to if instructions are inappropriate?

"Principle 4 – you act with honesty"

This principle feels as if it should be familiar, but it was newly introduced as a fundamental tenet of ethical behaviour in November 2019. Never before had it been considered necessary to state the blindingly obvious although, of course, there have always been a very small percentage of dishonest solicitors who have had their come-uppance before the Solicitors Disciplinary Tribunal (SDT). Dishonest solicitors are rarely given a second chance, such is the gravity of the situation in which they find themselves.

Honesty was added in 2019 as a standalone duty to support SRA regulatory work and to ensure that the right message was given to members of the public. The test applied when considering dishonesty develops from the thinking in the case of *Ivey v Genting Casinos (UK) Ltd t/a Crockfords*[20] so that a two-fold consideration of conduct is set as follows:

1. What was the individual's genuine knowledge or belief as to the facts at the time?
2. In view of their knowledge or belief at the time, was their conduct dishonest by the standards of ordinary decent people?

The SRA cites the following as examples of dishonest conduct in breach of Principle 4: lying to or misleading a client or third party; using the court for false claims; helping others to act improperly, perhaps by giving credibility to dubious enterprises; misleading others; lying on CVs and similar documents; backdating or creating false documentation.[21]

As with the other basic ethical duties, Principle 4 requires in-house counsel to consider their own position first. It is not inconceivable that

---

20 *Ivey v Genting Casinos (UK) Ltd t/a Crockfords* [2017] UKSC 67.
21 SRA Guidance, 'Acting with honesty', www.sra.org.uk/solicitors/guidance/general-dishonesty/.

allegations of dishonesty in the workplace could arise through acting on client instructions. In other words, it is important to be satisfied that client instructions do not jeopardise your own position as a regulated individual. This might mean it is sensible to ensure that those providing instructions are made aware of counsel's boundaries and what is 'off limits' in terms of what will be done. It also means that it is prudent to be able to discuss improper instructions with senior colleagues and having access to the board level decision makers provides a safety net. While non-solicitors might not be motivated by the same considerations as lawyers, any investigation of an employee is likely to attract adverse publicity for the business and this is a persuasive argument for supporting counsel to challenge inappropriate behaviour.

The case of an in-house lawyer who facilitated sham property schemes while acting in legal roles in various companies is an extreme example of a breach of Principle 4.[22] In this case, the solicitor had added what the Solicitors Disciplinary Tribunal described as a "veneer of respectability" in respect of the marketing of off-plan plot sales to investors in a scam that amounted to a £16 million fraud. The solicitor involved claimed that he believed that the scheme was legitimate and/ or that he had acted under duress. The SDT found that he had acted dishonestly, and he was struck off the roll of solicitors and required to pay costs of £41,000.

Not all such acts of dishonesty originate in this type of wrongdoing. Acts of dishonesty can often have simpler origins in mistakes such as forgetting to ensure documentation is prepared in good time or witnessed correctly. Often this happens because of human error. It is important to understand that the SRA has little or no sympathy with unprincipled behaviour that is designed to remedy a mistake or acts of dishonesty where there was no personal benefit gained by the solicitor as a result. Senior in-house counsel will want to encourage a collegiate environment so that individuals feel able to be open about such mistakes.

---

22   SDT case 292328 re Timothy Peter Ackrel, 6 January 2020.

"Principle 5 – you act with integrity"

Honesty was added to the high-level ethical duties in 2019, whereas integrity is a value that has been included as a core value for a lot longer. It would be easy to be confused by the concepts of honesty and integrity as two separate behaviours, but the SRA explains the distinction in the following way:[23]

> *Whilst someone acting dishonestly can be said to be acting without integrity, the concept of integrity is wider than just acting dishonestly. In other words, this means that it is possible to behave without integrity, and face disciplinary repercussions, without necessarily being dishonest.*

These integrity and honesty deliberations have long been a bone of contention for many practitioners who have found themselves facing disciplinary wrath on the grounds of lack of integrity. For example, the distinction between integrity and dishonesty, and the overwhelming expectations that integrity imposes on regulated individuals, was a point under deliberation in the Court of Appeal in the matter of *Wingate and Evans v SRA; SRA v Malins*[24] in which it was established that dishonesty and lack of integrity were not synonymous and did not both need to be proved in disciplinary matters.

In the case of *Wingate*, a solicitor who was a partner in a law firm had signed a loan agreement in the knowledge that he would be unable to fulfil the contract but on the assumption that the contract would be superseded by a separate version. The SDT decided that the solicitor lacked integrity. In the case of *Malins*, a solicitor partner backdated a notice of funding in order to avoid the consequences of lack of insurance where the original notice had been lost. The solicitors were struck off the roll of solicitors for lack of integrity. The matters were appealed, and both were reconsidered by the High Court who found that dishonesty and

---

23 SRA Guidance, 'Acting with integrity', www.sra.org.uk/solicitors/guidance/acting-with-integrity/.

24 *Wingate and Evans v SRA; SRA v Malins* [2018] EWCA Civ 366.

lack of integrity were the same. As the SRA had not pleaded dishonesty these matters were reconsidered in the Court of Appeal.

The Court of Appeal considered whether integrity requires more than honesty. Lord Justice Jackson provided an interpretation which is now used to evaluate integrity. In his view, honesty was "a basic moral quality which is expected of all members of society". Integrity required more than this. Integrity was described by Jackson as being "more nebulous" but was a "useful shorthand to express the higher standards which society expects from professional persons and which the professions expect from their own members" and that "[i]ntegrity connotes adherence to the ethical standards of one's own profession. That involves more than mere honesty. To take one example, a solicitor conducting negotiations or a barrister making submissions to a judge or arbitrator will take particular care not to mislead. Such a professional person is expected to be even more scrupulous about accuracy than a member of the public in daily discourse. The duty to act with integrity applies not only to what professional persons say, but to what they do."

The SRA provides examples of lack of integrity including making false representations on behalf of a client; recklessly misleading the court; taking unfair advantage of the client or third parties; knowingly or recklessly causing harm or distress to another or allowing clients or third parties to be misled.[25]

Like acts of dishonesty, often integrity issues arise in circumstances where the individual is unable to speak up or perhaps admit a mistake or a misunderstanding. Where the issue lies with a less experienced lawyer, the SRA is entitled to consider whether lack of effective supervision contributed to the breach. Senior in-house counsel should consider whether they create the right environment, with an appropriate support network, in which others can report mistakes, raise concerns and generally work in an open way. While the SRA is unable to challenge the

---

25   SRA Guidance, 'Acting with integrity', www.sra.org.uk/solicitors/guidance/acting-with-integrity/.

employer as to the circumstances that gave rise to a solicitor's lack of integrity, a senior in-house colleague could easily be asked to justify the supervision regime and explain how or why a junior colleague was able to act in an unprincipled way.

"Principle 6 – you act in a way that encourages equality, diversity and inclusion"

This Principle is used to enforce the SRA's regulatory objectives such as access to justice and the development of a diverse profession. You will be expected to demonstrate adherence to these values both in the workplace, in respect of your client and third parties and also in your personal lives.

The starting point will of course be compliance with the Equality Act 2010 but the SRA's expectations go beyond the minimum legal obligations so that regulatory duties require the demonstration of fairness and inclusivity.

In the in-house context, many businesses will have copious amounts of documentation to support equality and diversity. In-house counsel should use these as their starting point, but very critically assess them to see if they are suitable for the purposes of demonstrating compliance with SRA Principle 6. It might be necessary to add to, or alter, firmwide responses to meet the SRA requirements. In fact, many in-house legal departments draft their own team-wide equality, diversity and inclusivity policies to address SRA concerns. While the SRA would not expect in-house counsel to dictate equality responses to the rest of a business, there is the expectation that there will be a demonstration of personal accountability. For more senior in-house counsel this might take the form of influencing the board and senior colleagues so that, for example, recruitment and progression initiatives accommodate inclusivity initiatives. For junior in-house counsel, it will be the expectation that inappropriate behaviours, such as discriminatory behaviour or language, are challenged and concerns raised in a timely way.

In-house counsel should ask themselves:

- Do my employer's equality, diversity and inclusivity (EDI) initiatives foster the appropriate values?
- Can I rely on these EDI resources to also demonstrate compliance with Principle 6?
- Does the legal team need a bespoke suite of resources to address Principle 6 concerns and, if so, how do we make this happen?
- Are senior members of the team able to create an environment which both protects and promotes these behaviours?
- Is it possible to challenge inappropriate behaviours?
- Am I confident that complaints of unfair discrimination, such as those relating to sexual harassment, will be handled appropriately?
- Is training needed on equality legislation and/or the SRA's expectations?

It is essential that in-house counsel understand the severity with which allegations of inappropriate behaviour will be treated by the SRA, as shown by the following examples:

- A solicitor who routinely groped a secretary, made racist jokes and performed a Ku Klux Klan impersonation at her was fined £30,000, ordered to pay £21,000 costs and recommended by the SDT to undertake equality, diversity and inclusion training.[26]
- An "extremely drunk" senior solicitor was fined £10,000 for touching and kissing a paralegal.[27]

It is important to bear in mind that the SRA also expects to see equality, diversity and inclusivity behaviours being demonstrated in a solicitor's personal life. With this, there is an overlap between demonstrating adherence to Principle 6 with the values associated with

---

26 SDT case 12088-2020, re Samuel Maurice Charkham.
27 *The Law Society Gazette*, "'Drunk' senior partner touched paralegal inappropriately in front of colleagues", 22 July 2020, www.lawgazette.co.uk/news/drunk-senior-partner-touched-paralegal-inappropriately-in-front-of-colleagues/5105101.article.

Principle 2 and the duty to uphold public trust and confidence in the profession. The SRA expects self-reporting of any conduct where there is a serious breach of regulatory requirements and is likely to regard any incident involving discriminatory behaviour as worthy of investigation.

In 2019, a registered foreign lawyer was rebuked by the SRA and required to pay costs of £600. He had been found by an employment tribunal to have directly discriminated against his children's nanny and unfairly dismissed her. Amongst other findings, the SRA acknowledged that the case was unconnected with the individual's legal practice and that there was no lack of integrity in evidence, but that the act of discrimination had breached trust and confidence and that also he had breached his notification duties by failing to make a self-declaration to the SRA.[28]

"Principle 7 – you act in the best interests of each client"
This is an overly quoted expression and sentiment, but what does this Principle really mean? Guidance on the meaning has been provided over the years. For example, in the SRA Handbook, which was in force between 2011 and 2019, narrative to accompany this core principle stated: "You should always act in good faith and do your best for each of your clients."[29]

In practice, this requires an assessment of whether it is possible to promote the client's interests in a legally and ethically compliant way, and in a way that reinforces the fiduciary nature of the relationship between solicitor and client.

Key subject matters to be considered are as follows:

- Do I have a conflict (either an own interest or client conflict) of interests that prevents me from acting in my client's best interests?
- Can I uphold my duty of confidentiality to current and former clients?

---

28   In the matter of Sylvian Dhennin, Agreement dated 6 August 2019.
29   SRA Handbook, www.sra.org.uk/solicitors/handbook/.

- Can I disclose all material information to my current client?
- Am I able to act with competence and provide a proper standard of service?

At first glance, the in-house counsel might assume that these questions are relevant only in private practice. This is not the case; in-house counsel must remember that while their client base is noticeably less varied and more predictable than in private practice, they must test Principle 7 with each new matter in which they are asked to assist.

It is important to identify the client in each matter. Conflicts can arise in the in-house environment or there may be issues with competency or confidentiality and disclosure duties, and it would be a breach of Principle 7 to act in such circumstances. Where in-house counsel is unable to act in a client's best interests then the correct application of Principle 7 is to ensure that alternative service providers are sourced. The question which in-house counsel must be able to justify in each matter in which they are acting is whether they are satisfied that they are able to act in the client's best interests.

The regulatory interest in personal lives

The subject matter of the Principles ought not to come as a surprise to any solicitor. These are the basic values that support the collective reputation of the profession as trustworthy advisers and officers of the court.

The fact that the profession is expected to demonstrate principled behaviour outside of the workplace might be a more unexpected message but to ignore this point is a risk. Of course, the regulator is not interested in the totality of an individual's private life but is still able to exert regulatory reach over any behaviour that is likely to have an impact on professional perceptions. In guidance, the SRA makes statements to demonstrate their interest: "We do not expect everyone to conform to a perfect ideal of personal behaviour outside of practice. The threshold for us taking action relating to conduct in personal relationships is high but may well be crossed by unlawful or abusive behaviour" and "We will act where other conduct, either inside or outside of practice, would diminish the public's trust if they knew it was done by a solicitor ... This will include discriminatory conduct or behaviour involving violence or sexual harassment. We will always investigate where a criminal offence has been committed. The solicitor is likely to have breached Principle 2, given the key role they play in the administration of justice and the high degree of trust placed in solicitors and law firms by the public".[30]

THOUGHT LEADERSHIP

The following thought leader article is contributed by **Fergal Cathie,** *partner, and* **Michael Clark,** *legal director, of Clyde & Co LLP's professional disputes and regulatory group.*

In recent years, the SRA has increased its scrutiny of the solicitors' profession. It is now willing to pursue national and global firms as well as sole practitioners, 'big beast' City partners and junior associates and non-lawyers working in regulated firms. It has taken action against solicitors in relation to their conduct outside the office and against locally qualified lawyers in overseas offices. We have seen high-profile and lengthy trials and public settlements, leading to substantial fines and strike-offs, but also complete acquittals, the overturning of SDT decisions by the courts and – whatever the result of the prosecution itself – the potentially devastating impact of prosecutions on private lives and successful careers.

In-house lawyers are not immune from any of this. In this article, we consider some of the exposures to which they are subject.

---

30 SRA Guidance, 'Public trust and confidence', www.sra.org.uk/solicitors/guidance/public-trust-confidence/.

The SRA Standards and Regulations 2019

In November 2019, the SRA introduced a new Handbook, the SRA Standards and Regulations 2019, known colloquially as the 'STaRs'. This included a new set of seven Principles and two separate Codes of Conduct – one for firms and one for individual solicitors, RELs and RFLs. The regulatory regime is underpinned by a published Enforcement Strategy, which evolves over time. The Principles and the Code for individuals apply to all solicitors, including those working outside private practice in law firms or other business structures.[31]

By establishing two separate Codes, the SRA placed renewed emphasis on the need for individual solicitors to take responsibility for their own conduct. A law firm may be responsible for its systems and controls and the culture that it promotes, but it is for all individual solicitors to exercise their own judgement, act in accordance with the rules of their profession and be able to justify their decisions.

No matter how well integrated into the non-legal, commercial culture and activities of their workplace, in-house solicitors should not lose sight of this. Indeed, a number of the case studies which illustrate the SRA's published guidance on the Handbook include examples involving in-house solicitors (eg, the guidance on misleading the court). Further, solicitors who manage other individuals are obliged by the Code to ensure that they are "competent to carry out their role, and keep their professional knowledge and skills, as well as understanding of their legal, ethical and regulatory obligations, up to date".[32] It seems pretty clear that managers therefore have regulatory obligations to ensure that those whom they manage, which may include lawyers qualified in other

---

31   The Assessment of Character and Suitability Rules, the Authorisation of Individuals Regulations and the SRA Glossary also apply to in-house solicitors practising in England & Wales.

32   SRA Code of Conduct for Solicitors, Registered European Lawyers and Registered Foreign Lawyers, paragraph 3.6, www.sra.org.uk/solicitors/standards-regulations/code-conduct-solicitors/.

jurisdictions, other regulated persons (such as accountants) and support staff, all understand their obligations and work together to comply with them.

As well as the emphasis on individual responsibility, it is also striking that the Standards and Regulations take a less prescriptive approach to compliance than the previous Handbook. There is a much greater focus on individual standards and ethical behaviour, as part of a campaign to promote the concept that the solicitor 'brand' is one which can be trusted through and through. At the heart of this is the concept of 'integrity'.

In *Wingate & Evans v SRA*, Lord Justice Jackson distinguished between honesty, "a basic moral quality which is expected of all members of society", and integrity, which he said was "a useful shorthand to express the higher standards which society expects from professional persons and which the professions expect from their own members". The SRA's decision to reinforce the need to take individual responsibility reflects this thinking and marks a shift away from 'compliance' (which many regard as a corporate responsibility) and back to ethics. It is a return to the traditional view that solicitors ought to be trusted 'to the ends of the earth', that they should feel privileged to be associated with the brand, in return for the higher standards to which they adhere. But how exactly are those standards to be measured? And where is the line to be drawn between conduct in the course of providing legal services – doing the job – and one's behaviour outside the workplace?

In its judgment on the appeal of a former Magic Circle law firm partner, who had been fined £35,000 by the SDT for misconducting himself in the context of a sexual encounter with a colleague,[33] the High Court stated that the solicitor's adherence to moral and ethical principles must:

---

33 *Ryan Beckwith v Solicitors Regulatory Authority* [2020] EWHC 3231 (Admin).

be applied within the context of the relevant statutory framework ... to the extent that there are applicable ethical standards they must be found in or derived from those rules ... The requirement to act with integrity must comprise identifiable standards. There is no free-standing legal notion of integrity in the manner of the received standard of dishonesty; no off-the-shelf standard that can be readily known by the profession and predictably applied.

That was a judgment on its own facts, but it reinforces the notion that solicitors do not need to be objective paragons of virtue: their conduct, at work and in private, should be judged by the regulator according to the established ethical framework of the profession. It also seems that serious breach of an important provision of the Code, or reckless disregard for it, might – in addition – lead to a finding of lack of integrity.

But what aspects of a solicitor's private life is it legitimate for the SRA to scrutinise?

As the Enforcement Strategy[34] states, *"our Principles set out the core ethical values we require of all those we regulate and apply at all times and in all contexts – and apply both in and outside of practice (as the context permits)"*. However, the SRA qualifies this as follows: *"We are concerned with the impact of conduct outside of legal practice including in the private lives of those we regulate if this touches on risk to the delivery of safe legal services in future. The closer any behaviour is to professional activities, or a reflection of how a solicitor might behave in a professional context, the more seriously we are likely to view it."*

In addition, in its Guidance on Public Trust and Confidence,[35] the SRA states that it *"will act where other conduct, either inside or outside*

---

34   www.sra.org.uk/sra/corporate-strategy/sra-enforcement-strategy/.
35   www.sra.org.uk/solicitors/guidance/public-trust-confidence/.

of practice, would diminish the public's trust if they knew it was done by a solicitor or by someone in an SRA-regulated firm. This will include discriminatory conduct or behaviour involving violence or sexual harassment".

Thus, the SRA says that it may take action in relation to conduct in a solicitor's private life where it exposes a risk to the practice of law or the reputation of the profession (eg, criminal conduct) or where the conduct is not criminal or obviously unacceptable but might nevertheless undermine public trust in the profession.

Applying such an approach in practice is a challenge, and we can expect to see changes of emphasis as wider cultural and societal changes take place. On the face of it, the scope for SRA scrutiny seems limitless: all sorts of lawful behaviour may not be obviously acceptable but may nevertheless seem distasteful or unpleasant to many, and therefore capable of undermining 'public trust'. However, a number of SDT prosecutions in relation to conduct under the pre-2019 regime give a flavour of the types of private behaviour which the SRA has been prepared to put to the test.

At one end of the spectrum are cases involving criminal convictions where some sort of professional sanction is unsurprising.

For example, in 2017, an in-house solicitor was convicted of assault and racially aggravated assault against a former girlfriend, which he had committed while drunk. The solicitor was made subject to a community service order and a restraining order. This led to a hearing before the SDT and a subsequent appeal in the High Court. Ultimately, the solicitor was suspended for two years from the date of the SDT hearing.

Then we see the cases involving solicitors sending offensive communications (on which there is separate SRA Guidance), including via social media. Such communications have included anti-Semitic and misogynistic comments on Facebook, and tweets expressing hostility towards Islam, Catholicism and Judaism.

Similarly, in 2018, a solicitor who did not hold a current practising certificate and was employed as a paralegal by the General Medical Council was fined £5,000 by the SDT for sending highly offensive, racist and discriminatory messages to a colleague via his employer's instant messaging system. A fine was imposed, which would have been substantially higher had the respondent's culpability not been mitigated by a medical condition and the impact of medication.

It is unsurprising that sanctions including fines and suspension have been imposed in these cases. Perhaps more surprising to some will be the case of the partner in a City law firm who was rebuked by the SRA for having breached the old Principle 6 (behaving in a way that maintains the trust the public places in the profession and in the provision of legal services), after it was found in employment tribunal proceedings that he had discriminated against his children's nanny and unfairly dismissed her. Commentators have questioned what this episode from the solicitor's private home life had to do with the SRA, but it exemplifies a hard-line approach to discrimination, at work and in private, which chimes with a renewed emphasis on upholding equality, diversity and inclusion.

More nuanced, and certainly capable of generating controversy from many perspectives, is the case of the former Magic Circle partner, referred to above, who was involved in a sexual liaison with a colleague. Aspects of the conduct in question may have seemed distasteful or unpleasant to some, and the SDT – imposing a fine of £35,000 – considered that the respondent had lacked integrity and had not behaved in a way that maintained the public trust. But the High Court overturned that judgment on appeal. Also, while seriously abusive conduct by a member of the profession would clearly be capable of damaging the public trust in the provision of legal services – damaging the 'brand' – that conclusion was not supported by the facts. There was, the court said, a qualitative distinction between conduct affecting the respondent's personal reputation and conduct affecting his reputation as a provider of legal services or the reputation of his profession. On any view, this is uncertain territory, and it remains to be seen how the SRA will seek to define the boundaries as society continues to respond to the diversity and inclusion agenda.

The key message to be derived from all of this is that all solicitors – however they are employed – should bear in mind the privileged status they hold and therefore strive to uphold ethical standards in all they do, including in their private lives. The renewed emphasis on individual responsibility, whatever one's level of seniority and wherever one works, means that the in-house community needs to be just as well equipped as those in private practice.

Top tips to support compliance with the Principles
- ✔ Ensure that your employer is aware of your need to comply with the Principles.
- ✔ Understand that if a conflict arises in respect of application of the Principles, public interest duties – such as the rule of law, trust and confidence, acting with integrity – must be prioritised.
- ✔ Consider the relevance of the Principles in your private life and be aware of risk hot spots such as personal social media misuse.
- ✔ In senior roles, ensure all solicitor colleagues are aware of the Principles and their application in both their professional and private life, and develop a team culture that facilitates compliance.
- ✔ In senior roles, ensure colleagues are confident both to admit to mistakes and to call out inappropriate behaviours.
- ✔ Keep up to date with disciplinary work by reading the *Law Society Gazette* for reports of SRA and SDT enforcement action.

Chapter V:

Sources of ethical knowledge for in-house counsel (2)

SRA Code of Conduct for Solicitors, Registered European Lawyers and Registered Foreign Lawyers

---

The STaRs include a further source of ethical behaviours in a section called the SRA Code of Conduct for Solicitors, Registered European Lawyers (RELs) and Registered Foreign Lawyers (RFLs) (the SRA Code). These are the three types of lawyers with whom the SRA has a direct regulatory interest, and this SRA Code applies to them personally.

The SRA says that the SRA Code "describes the standards of professionalism that we, the SRA, and the public expect of individuals (solicitors, RELs and RFLs) authorised by us to provide legal services. They apply to conduct and behaviour relating to your practice and comprise a framework for ethical and competent practice which applies irrespective of your role or the environment or organisation in which you work".[1]

The SRA Code adds flesh to the bones of the SRA Principles and explains the ethical objectives which must be achieved in the working environment and in connection with the provision of legal services. The style of the Code might be a surprise to in-house counsel who have not kept up to speed with regulation. The SRA Code contains standards of professionalism rather than a series of prescriptive rules. This means that much of the tone is objective-setting and aspirational.

In other words, the SRA requires individuals to assess which standards are relevant, and therefore must be achieved, in any given scenario and ensure that this happens. How this happens is not specified in the text, leaving individuals to assess for themselves what might be appropriate in their particular environment. The clue that this is expected is in the language used in the introduction; the SRA says that you must exercise your judgement in applying these standards and take into account variables such as your role and responsibilities, areas of practice etc. You are personally accountable for compliance and must always be prepared to justify decisions.

Phrasing such as this – judgement, accountability and justifying – places an enormous responsibility on the individual who is regulated. The SRA Code should be viewed as a personal toolkit which the individual solicitor (and REL and RFL) must use to ensure that the correct ethical stance is adopted but in the knowledge that this toolkit will also be used as a means of testing compliance and assessing behaviour by the regulator.

The SRA Code applies to all forms of practice including in-house employment, and the myth that must be crushed is that the SRA will accept a light-touch response from in-house counsel. This response will not be tolerated. As has been described previously, the SRA is a

---

1   SRA Code of Conduct for Solicitors, Registered European Lawyers and Registered Foreign Lawyers, www.sra.org.uk/solicitors/standards-regulations/code-conduct-solicitors/.

"The SRA Code applies to all forms of practice including in-house employment, and the myth that must be crushed is that the SRA will accept a light-touch response from in-house counsel."

risk-based regulator whose reach must extend to all solicitors in all forms of practice. The SRA's work is driven less by client complaints (which are more likely to be brought to its attention in private practice) and more by the need to manage the profession's collective reputation as trustworthy providers of good quality and ethically based legal services.

In other words, there is a need for all in-house counsel to understand and apply the SRA Code to their particular form of practise. This triggers soul-searching. In-house counsel's response to the SRA Code will be determined by such factors as an individual's role and responsibilities; more senior counsel will be expected to be able to contribute more to the business ethos and to influence the ethical spirit of their legal team while junior colleagues, not yet in influential roles, must know their own individual ethical responsibilities, yet be ready to challenge inappropriate behaviour when they witness it.

The correct response will also be determined by the type of legal services delivered so that, for example, being involved in dispute resolution requires compliance with standards relating to courts, tribunals and inquiries whereas non-contentious work will not. It is also determined by the client base. In the majority of cases, the client will be the employer, but it is possible to act for others in certain circumstances. The SRA describes this as providing services to the public or a section of the public and the SRA Code contains requirements relating to client care, complaints handling and publicity which must be met in these circumstances.

Bearing in mind the accountability and justification expectations, it is important to adopt appropriate ways to demonstrate compliance. Again, how we demonstrate effective compliance in practice is not prescribed by the SRA and we are left to respond to this expectation in a way which suits our needs and our business. Senior in-house counsel will want to consider the conversations which must be had with other parts of the business so that there is an understanding about how legal services will be provided.

Senior counsel with responsibilities for legal teams might want to consider the appropriateness of existing business policies and, if necessary, introduce a bespoke legal team compliance system with policies, controls and procedures designed to support compliance with the SRA Code. Junior counsel will want to ensure that these policies are appropriate for them and that they are therefore able to demonstrate compliance. They need to know who to raise concerns with and when and how to seek help with ethical and regulatory concerns. Lone counsel are less likely to need a set of documented policies and instead need to develop ways of working that provide them with sufficient evidence that they are not a regulatory risk.

The standards in the SRA Code are described below with a commentary as to application and suggestions about how compliance can be demonstrated.

"Chapter 1 – Maintaining trust and acting fairly"

This chapter deals with ethical behaviours which arise in connection with Principle 1 (the rule of law and proper administration of justice), Principle 2 (trust and confidence) and Principle 6 (equality, diversity and inclusion). These are public interest principles; compliance with these is necessary for maintenance of the profession's collective reputation as trustworthy providers of legal services. The paragraphs in Chapter 1 answer questions which might arise if there is a tension between these Principles and your personal position and/or instructions given by your client.

"Chapter 2 – Dispute resolution and proceedings before courts, tribunals and inquiries"

This chapter describes our ethical boundaries when using court services. As such, and for in-house counsel, who provide dispute resolution services, there ought not be any surprises as to the content of the chapter. Pressures might arise because of client instructions, in particular, where these instructions are given to less experienced colleagues. It is

Table 2: Compliance considerations and strategies

Reference	Wording	Commentary	Compliance suggestions
1.1	"You do not unfairly discriminate by allowing your personal views to affect your professional relationships and the way in which you provide your services."	This paragraph makes it clear that regulatory requirements extend beyond compliance with equality legislation. Personal views should not be allowed to fetter the way in which we deal with clients and others with whom we have a professional relationship, nor should the way in which we provide legal services be affected.	• Induction training • Assessment of business policy and, if necessary, appropriate legal team EDI policy which supports compliance with this paragraph • Training on Equality Act 2010 and bolt-on topics such as those relating to unconscious bias, interview skills etc • Whistleblowing or similar policy • Complaints policy
1.2	"You do not abuse your position by taking unfair advantage of clients or others."	This supports Principle 2 and is designed to promote trust and confidence in the profession and address any concerns of unfair advantage that might be caused by information asymmetry. Particular pinch points for in-house counsel might be when communicating with third parties on behalf of the client, such as when acting in debt recovery and dispute resolution work.	• Training on communication skills • Template wording to ensure third parties are advised to seek legal assistance etc

continued on next page

Reference	Wording	Commentary	Compliance suggestions
1.3	"You perform all *undertakings* given by you, and do so within an agreed timescale or if no timescale has been agreed then within a reasonable amount of time."	"An undertaking is a statement, given orally or in writing, whether or not it includes the word 'undertake' or 'undertaking', to someone who reasonably places reliance on it, that you or a third party will do something or cause something to be done, or refrain from doing something." Breach of an undertaking is a serious regulatory event. If a promise is made and broken, this undermines trust and confidence in the standing of the solicitor. For this reason, there is no expectation that a solicitor will give an undertaking unless they are satisfied that their personal position is not compromised. In-house counsel are advised to think carefully about the implications of giving an undertaking, even if this is for and on behalf of their client, unless they are satisfied that they are fully indemnified by their client and that they are able to personally perform the undertaking.	• Undertakings policy – who can give an undertaking; wording and style to be used; sign-off required; and records to be maintained • Register for undertakings received by third parties • Documented discussion with the business to ensure counsel's position is understood

continued on next page

Reference	Wording	Commentary	Compliance suggestions
1.4	"You do not mislead or attempt to mislead your *clients*, the *court* or others, either by your own acts or omissions or allowing or being complicit in the acts or omissions of others (including your *client*)."	This paragraph builds on the preceding ethical objectives in this chapter. As officers of the court, and members of a trusted profession, solicitors must not personally, and must not be used by others to deceive others or misrepresent any matter, and face serious consequences if this paragraph is breached. Examples of improper behaviour that the SRA has considered in this context include knowing that a client has obtained information by illegal means but assisting the client to provide a false explanation to disguise this fact.	• Documented discussion with the business to ensure that counsel's position is understood

important that every member of the in-house legal team understands what is expected in respect of duties to the court and knows that they can, and indeed must, challenge inappropriate behaviour. These are significant duties; behaving unethically in court room scenarios is likely to lead to complaints being brought to the attention of the SRA by the judiciary and can also result in negative media attention for the individual, for the employer and for the SRA.

These duties have given rise to a particularly infamous SDT ruling involving an in-house solicitor when an individual was alleged to have allowed a court to be misled and thereby failed to act with integrity. This is the case brought against Alastair Brett. Mr Brett was in-house counsel at the *Times* newspaper and during the Leveson Inquiry was found to have caused or allowed a witness statement to be used which knowingly or recklessly created a misleading impression as to the facts in this statement. The SDT considered the circumstances and found that Mr Brett had not prioritised his duties to the court. He was suspended from practice for a period of time. Although Mr Brett appealed the decision of the SDT and was partially successful in challenging some of the wording of its findings, his suspension was nonetheless maintained.[2]

Table 3: Compliance considerations and strategies

Reference	Wording	Commentary	Compliance suggestions
2.1	"You do not misuse or tamper with evidence or attempt to do so."	Clearly, such actions are likely to be regarded as incompatible with principled behaviour such as acting with honesty and acting with integrity.	• Training of all relevant staff • Documented discussions with the business to ensure its understanding of what can be asked of counsel
2.2	"You do not seek to influence the substance of evidence, including generating false evidence or persuading witnesses to change their evidence."	An example of behaviour that is likely to indicate a breach include attempts to persuade expert witnesses to alter reports for the client's benefit.	• As above

continued on next page

---

2   *Brett v SRA* [2014] EWHC 2974 (Admin).

Reference	Wording	Commentary	Compliance suggestions
2.3	"You do not provide or offer to provide any benefit to witnesses dependent upon the nature of their evidence or the outcome of the case."	While it is not improper to pay reasonable expenses to witnesses, a payment dependent on the outcome of a case would be unethical.	• As above, plus effective supervision to monitor for compliance
2.4	"You only make assertions or put forward statements, representations or submissions to the *court* or others which are properly arguable."	The SRA has been critical of misuse of the court processes by this means. As officers of the court, solicitors are required to consider what is appropriate.	• As above
2.5	"You do not place yourself in contempt of *court*, and you comply with *court* orders which place obligations on you."	As officers of the court, in-house counsel have a duty to comply with court orders made against them.	• Documented discussions so that the business understands counsel's position
2.6	"You do not waste the *court's* time."	The SRA asks that claims are made properly and honestly. All solicitors must remember not only their duties to clients, but also their overriding duties to the court, and to the rule of law and the proper administration of justice. In recent years, the SRA has flagged its concerns	• As above

continued on next page

Reference	Wording	Commentary	Compliance suggestions
		with misuse of court time in connection with improper holiday sickness claims, payment protection insurance claims and certain types of personal injury instructions. While these particular subjects are unlikely to be relevant to in-house counsel, it must be remembered that use of the court must be for proper purposes. Abuse of the litigation process is also criticised, and this might be a concern for in-house counsel. This involves the use or threat of litigation for inappropriate reasons such as causing detriment or distraction to business competitors etc.	
2.7	"You draw the *court's* attention to relevant cases and statutory provisions, or procedural irregularities of which you are aware, and which are likely to have a material effect on the outcome of the proceedings."	This behaviour ties in with duties as officers of the court. The court must be informed of relevant cases and statutory provisions by the litigators on both sides of a matter.	• This duty might seem counterintuitive but must be understood • Training • Supervision • Discussions with the business

"Chapter 3 – Service and competence"

This chapter of the SRA Code deals with service delivery and service standards with requirements relating to taking client instructions, ensuring competency and effective supervision. At first glance, none of this might seem relevant to in-house counsel, particularly if their client base is restricted to providing services only to their employer. This is not so.

In-house counsel are in the same position as private practitioners in that they can act only on properly provided instructions. This means it is vital to know who is able to provide these instructions and thereby alter the client's position.

It is also necessary to consider competency and to be competent, both from the angle that this must be affirmed to the SRA when requesting that a practising certificate is renewed and also from the perspective of being satisfied that the services demonstrate a proper level of knowledge and they are delivered in a timely fashion.

Finally, this chapter sets out the SRA's demanding expectations about supervision in the workplace and makes solicitor supervisors personally accountable for the services provided by others under their care.

With the paragraphs in this chapter, there will be a need to assess the dynamics of the legal team and the relationship with the business. Again, there are different roles for different members of the team; senior counsel will need to take the lead in terms of reaching agreement with the business about how new matters will be onboarded, and the form of supervision and competency training. With supervision and training, the starting point will be a consideration of the business-wide procedures and what should be adapted to deal with in-house counsel's regulatory considerations.

For junior in-house counsel, the response will be different; do they understand personal obligations such as to act only on properly given instructions, and do they compile the evidence to show that in changing the client's position they are acting ethically, that they contribute fully and openly to the supervisory process and that they take accountability for identifying training needs?

Table 4: Compliance considerations and strategies

Reference	Wording	Commentary	Compliance suggestions
3.1	"You only act for *clients* on instructions from the *client*, or from someone properly authorised to provide instructions on their behalf. If you have reason to suspect that the instructions do not represent your *client's* wishes, you do not act unless you have satisfied yourself that they do. However, in circumstances where you have legal authority to act notwithstanding that it is not possible to obtain or ascertain the instructions of your *client*, then you are subject to the overriding obligation to protect your *client's* best interests."	It is too easy to assume that client identification is a straightforward task. The SRA's definition is that a client is the person for whom you act. This can be different from the individual who provides instructions and/or it should not be assumed that the person with whom you are dealing has authority to bind the client to a particular course of action. It is unlikely that in-house counsel will not be able to take instructions from the client, or someone properly authorised, as this envisages the type of situation where Public Guardian's Office might be involved and similar.	• Documented discussion with the business to ensure that there is agreement about who is authorised to provide instructions and any limits to their authority • Template client inception/new matter form so that client and instructing party can be recorded

continued on next page

Reference	Wording	Commentary	Compliance suggestions
3.2 3.3	"You ensure that the service you provide to *clients* is competent and delivered in a timely manner." "You maintain your competence to carry out your role and keep your professional knowledge and skills up to date."	These paragraphs require in-house counsel to be satisfied on a number of matters: • Do I have the legal knowledge to provide a proper standard of service? • Am I keeping my legal knowledge up to date? • Have I considered other competencies such as the ability to communicate effectively? • Do I have adequate time to meet appropriate service standards? • Do I have suitable resources (eg, help from support staff, appropriate facilities)?	• Assessment of the suitability of business's learning and development resources, and agreement if these need to be topped up to accommodate the needs of in-house counsel • Training policy • Training records • Whistleblowing policy (to address any concerns about resources etc)
3.4	"You consider and take account of your *client's* attributes, needs and circumstances."	Legal services must be delivered in a way that suits the needs of the client. In private practice, why this should be considered and how this is demonstrated will be	• Documented discussion with the business to ensure that there is agreement about means of delivering services coupled

continued on next page

Reference	Wording	Commentary	Compliance suggestions
		more obvious bearing in mind the diversity of the client base and the vulnerabilities that might be present. In the context of in-house practice, it is less likely that your client will be considered vulnerable, although bear in mind that we need to consider not only a client's characteristics but also their situation and the reason why they are seeking legal services. It is also necessary to consider how your client requires services to be delivered; the form of communication, the timing etc.	with internal team policy about documentation requirements for file management purposes (eg, attendance notes etc)
3.5	"Where you supervise or manage others providing legal services: (a) you remain accountable for the work carried out through them; and (b) you effectively supervise work being done for *clients*."	The regulator regards effective supervision as a fundamental element in the delivery of good quality and ethically based legal services, and this paragraph is used as a means of ensuring that this job is treated seriously.	• Assessment of the suitability of the business's supervisory arrangements and agreement if these need to be topped up to accommodate the needs of in-house counsel

continued on next page

Reference	Wording	Commentary	Compliance suggestions
		Note the key words in the paragraph; if you are a supervisor then you are *accountable* and you must *effectively* supervise; in other words, if a regulatory issue arises (perhaps a supervised individual has misled the court or failed to deliver a competent service to the client), this paragraph enables the regulator to draw the supervisor into the discussion about why this has happened. Note also the inference that everyone providing legal services should be supervised or managed. The way in which supervision is put into practice will depend on the needs and attributes of the person who is supervised.	• Clear documentation about supervision lines and responsibilities • Process to provide documented evidence of supervision, eg, requirement to have written notes of meetings, file review and appraisal processes • Supervision policy • Training for supervisors on soft skills such as effective communication strategies etc

continued on next page

Reference	Wording	Commentary	Compliance suggestions
3.6	"You ensure that the individuals you manage are competent to carry out their role, and keep their professional knowledge and skills, as well as understanding of their legal, ethical and regulatory obligations, up to date."	This places a personal responsibility on managers (which term is not defined for these purposes) to ensure competency standards are maintained. As with the wording in paragraph 3.5, take note that you are expected to *ensure* others are competent; you must guarantee or make sure that competency levels do not dip, and this might well mean that you are included in any conversations which the regulator has with other individuals if their competency is in question. Note also that competency extends beyond professional knowledge and skills to an up-to-date understanding of the individual's legal, ethical and regulatory obligations.	• Assessment of the suitability of the business's learning and development resources, with agreement reached about extra budget and resources which are needed to accommodate regulatory expectations • Clear documentation about management responsibilities (eg, who is considered to be a manager for these purposes) • Training policy and records

"Chapter 4 – Client money and assets"

This chapter is less likely to bother in-house counsel, as its primary aim is to protect and safeguard client money and this is almost exclusively relevant to private practitioners. However, if a holistic approach is taken,

Table 5: Compliance considerations and strategies

Reference	Wording	Commentary	Compliance suggestions
4.1	"You properly account to *clients* for any *financial benefit* you receive as a result of their instructions, except where they have agreed otherwise."	This is not likely to be relevant to in-house practice. A financial benefit includes commissions, discounts or rebates that you might receive.	N/A
4.2	"You safeguard money and *assets* entrusted to you by *clients* and others."	Asset is a defined term and includes "documents, wills, deeds, investments and other property".	• Understanding the business's safekeeping arrangements
4.3	"You do not personally hold *client money* save as permitted under regulation 10.2(b)(vii) of the Authorisation of Individuals Regulations, unless you work in an *authorised body*, or in an organisation of a kind *prescribed* under this rule on any terms that may be *prescribed* accordingly."	This paragraph sets out restrictions on holding client money. When working in an in-house counsel role, you are prohibited from holding client money unless working in a business which has been given this right by the SRA. This right is unlikely to be granted to a commercial business.	N/A

then in-house counsel will need to ensure that they do nothing which undermines their employer's financial position and/or assets.

"Chapter 5 – Referrals, introductions and separate businesses, and other business requirements"

This chapter contains a hotchpotch of regulatory duties and ethical requirements focusing on relationships with third parties, and the impact on the relationship with clients and other responsibilities relating to different types of working.

Table 6: Compliance considerations and strategies

Reference	Wording	Commentary	Compliance suggestions
5.1	"In respect of any referral of a *client* by you to another *person*, or of any third party who introduces business to you or with whom you share your *fees*, you ensure that: (a) *clients* are informed of any financial or other interest which you or your business or employer has in referring the *client* to another *person* or which an *introducer* has in referring the *client* to you; (b) *clients* are informed of any fee sharing arrangement that is relevant to their matter;	Referrals and introductions can create ethical difficulties in terms of compliance with SRA Principle 2 (trust and confidence), Principle 3 (independence) and Principle 7 (acting in the best interests of each client). Nothing about these arrangements should fetter the ability to advise the client impartially, and a number of conditions are attached to these relationships.	• If appropriate, a procedure to ensure that the conditions of this paragraph are met and evidenced

continued on next page

Reference	Wording	Commentary	Compliance suggestions
	(c) the fee sharing agreement is in writing; (d) you do not receive payments relating to a referral or make payments to an *introducer* in respect of *clients* who are the subject of criminal proceedings; and (e) any *client* referred by an *introducer* has not been acquired in a way which would breach the *SRA's regulatory arrangements* if the *person* acquiring the client were regulated by the *SRA*."	In practice, it is unlikely that in-house counsel will receive an introduction of business. However, it is not inconceivable that it might be necessary to refer the client to a third party for services (perhaps a firm of solicitors when the in-house legal team is unable to provide legal services) and in these circumstances it is necessary to comply with this paragraph.	
5.2	"Where it appears to the *SRA* that you have made or received a *referral fee*, the payment will be treated as a *referral fee* unless you show that the payment was not made as such."	There are legal prohibitions on the payment of referral fees and the SRA will expect you to satisfy it that you are not making an illegal payment.	N/A
5.3	"You only: (a) refer, recommend or introduce a *client* to a *separate business*; or (b) divide, or allow to be divided, a *client's* matter between you and a *separate business*; where the *client* has given informed consent to your doing so."	This will not be relevant to in-house counsel as it is a notification requirement that applies only in circumstances where you also practise through an authorised body (ie, private practice).	N/A

continued on next page

Reference	Wording	Commentary	Compliance suggestions
5.4	"You must not be a *manager, employee, member* or *interest holder* of a business that: (a) has a name which includes the word "solicitors"; or (b) describes its work in a way that suggests it is a *solicitors*' firm; unless it is an *authorised body*."	This is a prohibition which applies to all solicitors in that the word 'solicitors' must not be used in the name of any non-authorised business and nor must its work be described in a way that suggests it is a solicitors' firm.	N/A
5.5	"If you are a *solicitor* who holds a practising certificate, an *REL* or *RFL*, you must complete and deliver to the *SRA* an annual return in the *prescribed* form."	The regulatory requirement to hold a practising certificate and to ensure that it is renewed each year.	• In practice, it is important to ensure that your 'mySRA' details are accurate so that your certificate can be renewed through this online platform
5.6	"If you are a *solicitor* or an *REL* carrying on *reserved legal activities* in a *non-commercial body*, you must ensure that: (a) the body takes out and maintains indemnity insurance; and (b) this insurance provides adequate and appropriate cover in respect of the services that you provide or have provided, whether or not they comprise *reserved legal*	A non-commercial body is described in the Legal Services Act 2007 as a not-for-profit body, a community interest company or an independent trade union. Reserved legal activities are also described in this Act as meaning the exercise of a right of audience; the conduct of litigation;	• Only relevant to in-house counsel employed in non-commercial bodies, and performing reserved legal activities, but in such circumstances, arrangements must be made to ensure that existing

continued on next page

Reference	Wording	Commentary	Compliance suggestions
	activities, taking into account any alternative arrangements the body or its *clients* may make."	reserved instrument activities; probate activities; notarial activities; and the administration of oaths.	indemnity covers the provision of these legal services or that this type of indemnity is obtained

"Chapter 6 – Conflict, confidentiality and disclosure"

When asked about conflicts (either in the context of a conflict of interests or the type which arises where there is a conflict of duties such that confidentiality and disclosure requirements cannot be reconciled), the common assumption of many in-house counsel is that this is a private practice issue and not relevant to them because of their limited client base.

In fact, every solicitor, irrespective of the type of practice in which they are employed, must be alert to the possibility that a conflict of interests can arise, that they might breach confidentiality or that they will not be able to make full disclosure of material information. It is simply not true that these do not apply to in-house practice. Conflicts arise more often than is usually imagined.

Examples that can arise in the in-house arena include the following scenarios:

- Acting on instructions from an employer/client to deal with employment issues and unable to act impartially because the instructions impact counsel's own terms of employment negatively – an own interest conflict.
- Acquiring an interest in the business and this making a difference to the way you advise on matters – an own interest conflict.
- Drafting a contract on behalf of both parties (perhaps a holding and a subsidiary company in the same group) and being unable to protect the interests of both parties – a conflict of interest (otherwise described as a client conflict).

- Breaching confidentiality duties which arise in connection with the provision of legal services perhaps because of leaks of information to other employees or overheard conversations etc – confidentiality breaches.
- Acting for a client (perhaps a subsidiary company in the same group as counsel's employer) but unable to disclose material information to them because of duties owed to another client or the employer – disclosure breaches.

These are basic ethical duties, and the SRA expects nothing less than our complete understanding, and application, of relevant paragraphs in the SRA Code. Nor does the regulator suffer fools gladly; a solicitor will face severe consequences for breaching these duties. Such is the level of regulatory concern, that guidance has been issued ('Unregulated organisations, conflict and confidentiality'[3]) and it is recommended that this is shared as necessary with employers so that these limitations on your practice are understood.

Consider the following examples of regulatory enforcement action when these basic ethical duties were breached:

- In 2019, two solicitors who acted for a client despite an own interest conflict being apparent were each ordered by the Solicitors Disciplinary Tribunal to pay a £10,000 fine and each also ordered to pay £25,000 costs.[4]
- In 2017, a solicitor agreed a regulatory settlement agreement with the SRA and voluntarily removed himself from the roll of solicitors after admitting (in a newspaper article published in 2016) that he had disclosed confidential information about a client's affairs in 1979 and then again between 1985–87.[5]

---

3 SRA Guidance, "Unregulated organisations, conflict and confidentiality", www.sra.org.uk/solicitors/guidance/unregulated-organisations-conflict-confidentiality/.
4 SDT Application 11907-2018.
5 *The Law Society Gazette*, "Retired solicitor ends career after historic breach of client confidentiality", 29 June 2017, www.lawgazette.co.uk/news/retired-solicitor-ends-career-after-historic-breach-of-client-confidentiality/5061780.article.

Table 7: Compliance considerations and strategies

Reference	Wording	Commentary	Compliance suggestions
6.1	"You do not act if there is an *own interest conflict* or a significant risk of such a conflict."	An own interest conflict means "any situation where your duty to act in the best interests of any client in relation to a matter conflicts, or there is a significant risk that it may conflict, with your own interests in relation to that or a related matter".[1] This definition means that both actual conflicts and scenarios where there is a significant risk of conflict must be considered. The meaning of significant is not explained, and this requires the exercise of your judgement; how possible is it that you will be unable to act in the client's best interests if you accept instructions? Examples of the sources of own interest conflicts include your financial interests, professional and personal relationships, personal interests, and where action or services are required because you have given incorrect advice etc.	• Most businesses have procedures designed to deal with own interest conflicts and some might also have a register of interests or similar. These should be assessed for compatibility with the SRA requirement (which is an absolute prohibition on acting) • If there are no existing policies, a conflict policy for the legal team • An own interests register • Training • Client/matter inception process which requires consideration of conflicts

continued on next page

Reference	Wording	Commentary	Compliance suggestions

6.2	"You do not act in relation to a matter or particular aspect of it if you have a *conflict of interest* or a significant risk of such a conflict in relation to that matter or aspect of it, unless:
	(a) the *clients* have a *substantially common interest* in relation to the matter or the aspect of it, as appropriate; or
	(b) the *clients* are *competing for the same objective*, and the conditions below are met, namely that:
	  i. all the *clients* have given informed consent, given or evidenced in writing, to you acting;
	  ii. where appropriate, you put in place effective safeguards to protect your *clients'* confidential information; and
		This paragraph relates to the type of conflict of interest that arises when acting for two or more clients.
		  The definition of conflict of interest is: "a situation where your separate duties to act in the best interests of two or more clients in relation to the same or a related matter conflict".[ii]
		  Where such a conflict, or a significant risk of one, is identified then the requirement is that you do not act unless one of two specific exceptions apply and prescribed conditions are met. These are the substantially common interest and the competing for the same objective exceptions. These both have defined meaning. A substantially common interest "means a situation where there is a clear common purpose between the clients and a strong consensus on how it is to be achieved" and competing for the same objective means "any situation in which two or more clients are competing for an 'objective' which, if attained by one client, will make that 'objective' unattainable to the other
			• This type of conflict consideration is unlikely to have been considered by the business as it is a conflict that arises in respect of solicitors' duties
			• In-house counsel must not accept instructions that place them in breach of their duties to act ethically, and it is prudent to manage an employer's expectations and to draft a conflict policy to regularise actions if conflicts are identified and a process for making decisions about the use of the substantially common interest exception (eg, decision maker and collection of documentation for audit trail purposes)
			• Training

continued on next page

Reference	Wording	Commentary	Compliance suggestions
	iii. you are satisfied it is reasonable for you to act for all the *clients*."	client or clients, and 'objective' means an asset, contract or business opportunity which two or more clients are seeking to acquire or recover through a liquidation (or some other form of insolvency process) or by means of an auction or tender process or a bid or offer, but not a public takeover".[iii] It seems unlikely that in-house counsel will need to consider the competing for the same objective scenario, but the substantially common interest exception is likely to be more commonplace. For example, if asked to act for two or more clients (related companies in a group organisation etc) in contract negotiations, and in a situation where all terms have been agreed, then it would be possible to consider using the substantially common interest exception to act for both sides.	• Client/matter inception process which requires consideration of conflicts
6.3	"You keep the affairs of current and former *clients* confidential unless disclosure is required or permitted by law or the *client* consents."	This is the foundation stone upon which the successful solicitor-client relationship is built. It supports Principle 2 (trust and confidence), Principle 5 (integrity) and, of course,	• Most businesses have confidentiality requirements designed to ensure that business-sensitive

continued on next page

Reference	Wording	Commentary	Compliance suggestions
		Principle 7 (acting in the best interests of each client). The duty means that each client you currently or previously acted for, can expect their affairs to be kept confidential unless they waive this themselves or in circumstances where there is a legal obligation to make a disclosure. In some cases, this duty is also owed to prospective clients, but this particular stand does not appear to be particularly relevant to in-house counsel. For in-house counsel, this duty means it is essential to correctly identify the client in each matter they are instructed to act on so that the duty is bestowed on the correct entity. Put another way, when acting for someone who is not also your employer, it must be remembered that your duty of confidentiality would ordinarily prevent you from sharing any information with your employer, regardless of any expectations that might arise because of this contractual arrangement.	information is not lost or leaked. This policy is unlikely to cover the confidentiality duties which a solicitor employed in the business owes their client. It would be prudent to have discussions with the employer so that their expectations are managed and so that any necessary practical steps can be added to the business's processes (for example, ensuring that the legal team work in a suitable area of the office space and have secure IT resources etc) • Confidentiality policy • Training

continued on next page

Reference	Wording	Commentary	Compliance suggestions
		In practical terms, breach of the duty might be attributed to ways of working so consideration must be given to shared office space and IT systems. Care must be taken and discussions about legal instructions with other employees is wrong. Similarly, working away from the office needs to be managed carefully to avoid inadvertent breaches, such as loss of paperwork or overheard conversations.	
6.4	"Where you are acting for a *client* on a matter, you make the *client* aware of all information material to the matter of which you have knowledge, except when: (a) the disclosure of the information is prohibited by legal restrictions imposed in the interests of national security or the prevention of crime; (b) your *client* gives informed consent, given	This is a duty requiring solicitors to make full disclosure of material information to their clients in matters in which they are currently retained to provide legal services. This duty is imposed so that the client is able to give informed instructions. Material information is not defined but common sense dictates that this is information which is relevant to the matter in hand rather than information which is simply interesting or inconsequential. The decision about materiality is a matter for your judgement.	• This duty, and the qualifications, must be understood by in-house counsel's clients • Confidentiality policy should add process for dealing with the conflict of duties that may arise • Training (NB this duty, and the conflict with confidentiality, is often misunderstood)

continued on next page

Reference	Wording	Commentary	Compliance suggestions
	or evidenced in writing, to the information not being disclosed to them; (c) you have reason to believe that serious physical or mental injury will be caused to your *client* or another if the information is disclosed; or (d) the information is contained in a privileged document that you have knowledge of only because it has been mistakenly disclosed."	This duty is not absolute as can be seen by the exceptions included in the narrative of the paragraph. However, justifying use of any of the exceptions is not without risk, and reasons ought to be well-documented. Problems will arise in circumstances where the duty of disclosure cannot be reconciled with the duty of confidentiality in paragraph 6.3 of the SRA Code. In these circumstances, confidentiality duties take precedence and information must be protected. In-house counsel would be unable to continue acting, and the instructions would need to be transferred to someone else without the material information, or even mean that the instructions should be handled by external solicitors.	
6.5	"You do not act for a *client* in a matter where that *client* has an interest adverse to the interest of another current or former *client* of you or your business or employer, for	This deals with a particular type of scenario in which the duty of confidentiality and the duty of disclosure might not be reconcilable. The scenario in question is one in which the current client has an interest adverse to the former	• Given the nature of in-house practice it seems unlikely that this type of conflict of duties would arise

continued on next page

Reference	Wording	Commentary	Compliance suggestions
	whom you or your business or employer holds confidential information which is material to that matter, unless: (a) effective measures have been taken which result in there being no real risk of disclosure of the confidential information; or (b) the current or former *client* whose information you or your business or employer holds has given informed consent, given or evidenced in writing, to you acting, including to any measures taken to protect their information."	or other client to whom confidentiality is owed. The risks of acting in these circumstances are obvious and there have been some high-profile court cases, and SRA regulatory action, which have arisen where the decision to act has been questioned.	

i SRA Glossary, www.sra.org.uk/solicitors/standards-regulations/glossary/.
ii SRA Glossary, www.sra.org.uk/solicitors/standards-regulations/glossary/.
iii SRA Glossary, www.sra.org.uk/solicitors/standards-regulations/glossary/.

"Chapter 7 – Cooperation and accountability"

The paragraphs in this chapter clarify the SRA's expectations of a regulated individual and when and how interactions should take place.

The requirements are expected to influence the way in which the solicitor works, and includes the individual responsibility to communicate with the SRA. The clues about this are found in the title of the chapter; solicitors are required to cooperate, both in terms of proactively managing their legal persona and in terms of being forthcoming with information that is relevant to the regulator's opinion of them and the decision to allow them to practise. Cooperation also includes the obligation to respond to all enquiries made of them, of course, including the SRA's enquiries, but also from other interested stakeholders.

Table 8: Compliance considerations and strategies

Reference	Wording	Commentary	Compliance suggestions
7.1	"You keep up to date with and follow the law and regulation governing the way you work."	This paragraph interplays with competency requirements and the need to be able to provide good quality services with an understanding of the regulatory framework.	• Securing understanding and agreement of your employer about legal training needs • Identification of particular legal updating necessary for an individual's experience and role • Training programme and training budget • Training on SRA regulation, and updating as necessary

continued on next page

Reference	Wording	Commentary	Compliance suggestions
7.2	"You are able to justify your decisions and actions in order to demonstrate compliance with your obligations under the *SRA's regulatory arrangements*."	In other words, you can show that you have complied with professional and ethical duties when performing your role. Note the deliberate use of the word 'justify' here; to justify means that you must show that there was a good reason for your actions or that it was reasonable to act in a particular way. The SRA will put an individual to the test if there are queries about their behaviours and expect them to justify their actions.	• This paragraph suggests that it is prudent to have a consistent methodology to record decision making. The simplest way of doing this will be through attendance and file notes which capture contemporaneous thinking. Confirmatory emails and correspondence with clients showing their instructions, and your next steps, are also sensible. The client file should be a full and detailed history of the lifecycle of the matter
7.3	"You cooperate with the *SRA*, other regulators, ombudsmen, and those bodies with a role overseeing and supervising the delivery of, or investigating concerns in relation to, legal services."	A professional person is expected to demonstrate accountability not only to their own regulator but also to those other external stakeholders who have, for whatever reason, an interest in their actions.	• Ensuring that your employer understands that in some circumstances in-house counsel would be required to assist outside agencies

continued on next page

Reference	Wording	Commentary	Compliance suggestions
		This description will include any regulatory oversight bodies for the industry in which you are employed, the Information Commissioner's Office in respect of data protection issues, the National Crime Agency in respect of money laundering and related frauds, the Financial Conduct Authority and Prudential Regulation Authority in respect of financial services and of course the Legal Ombudsman for certain types of client complaints. Being uncooperative would be an indicator of unprincipled behaviour.	

continued on next page

Reference	Wording	Commentary	Compliance suggestions
7.4	"You respond promptly to the *SRA* and: (a) provide full and accurate explanations, information and documents in response to any request or requirement; and (b) ensure that relevant information which is held by you, or by third parties carrying out functions on your behalf which are critical to the delivery of your legal services, is available for inspection by the *SRA*."	This paragraph supports and develops the themes of cooperation and accountability contained in paragraph 7.3. The SRA is entitled to make enquiries of all regulated persons including those working in-house and require promptness and transparency from us.	• Again, it is important to ensure that the employer understands the SRA's entitlement to speak with in-house counsel in matters concerning their individual behaviours
7.5	"You do not attempt to prevent anyone from providing information to the *SRA* or any other body exercising regulatory, supervisory, investigatory or prosecutory functions in the public interest."	It would be a misuse of your position to attempt to prevent disclosure of information to external stakeholders or other bodies which might be investigating you. In practice, this is seen as a warning to those solicitors in	• Senior lawyers must understand this: non-disclosure agreements must be used with care

continued on next page

Reference	Wording	Commentary	Compliance suggestions
		positions of seniority and influence over others, such as the owners of law firms or senior members of legal teams who might seek to prevent others from whistleblowing or similar actions. This type of behaviour is not in the public interest and is therefore a regulatory concern.	
7.6	"You notify the *SRA* promptly if: (a) you are subject to any criminal charge, conviction or caution, subject to the Rehabilitation of Offenders Act 1974; (b) a *relevant insolvency event* occurs in relation to you; or (c) if you become aware:	The practising certificate renewal exercise gives the SRA an annual opportunity to consider your suitability to practise as a solicitor. This paragraph imposes a duty on you to make reports of certain events during the practising year, so that the SRA can promptly review the decision to grant a certificate.	• Reporting triggers might not be understood by in-house counsel and training on this regulatory duty is recommended • Induction process for new solicitor employees which includes attention to regulatory matters, and the need to update the practising address

continued on next page

Reference	Wording	Commentary	Compliance suggestions
	i. of any material changes to information previously provided to the *SRA*, by you or on your behalf, about you or your practice, including any change to information recorded in the *register*; and ii. that information provided to the *SRA*, by you or on your behalf, about you or your practice is or may be false, misleading, incomplete or inaccurate."	Note the wording of (a) and the need to report not only criminal convictions but also criminal charges and convictions. Guidance from the SRA's Enforcement Strategy indicates that where an individual notifies the regulator of any such matters themselves and at an earlier stage, then such communications are likely to be regarded as mitigating factors. Note also (c)(i) and the need to notify the SRA about practice changes. The SRA maintains a public register of practising addresses which must be kept up to date.	
7.7	"You report promptly to the *SRA* or another *approved regulator*, as appropriate, any facts or matters that you reasonably believe are capable of amounting to a serious breach of their *regulatory arrangements* by any *person*	All solicitors play a role in the risk-based regulatory work of the SRA so that they will be expected to report themselves and also other solicitors and registered foreign lawyers (and in private practice, also non-solicitor employees) if they	• Ensuring that your employer and other colleagues understand this duty • Training • Whistleblowing policy • Internal procedure to ensure that senior in-house counsel are notified of all such issues

continued on next page

Reference	Wording	Commentary	Compliance suggestions
	regulated by them (including you)."	believe that they have committed serious breaches of the SRA Standards and Regulations. This reporting duty also extends to matters that should be brought to the attention of other approved regulators. An approved regulator is a body approved to regulate legal service providers in England and Wales; the SRA, the Bar Standards Board, CILEx Regulation, Council for Licensed Conveyancers, Intellectual Property Regulation Board, Costs Lawyer Standards Board, Master of the Faculties and the ICAEW Probate Committee. Regulatory arrangements have a statutory meaning and include all the approved regulator's arrangements and rules that apply to the regulated individual.	

continued on next page

Reference	Wording	Commentary	Compliance suggestions
7.8	"Notwithstanding paragraph 7.7, you inform the *SRA* promptly of any facts or matters that you reasonably believe should be brought to its attention in order that it may investigate whether a serious breach of its *regulatory arrangements* has occurred or otherwise exercise its regulatory powers."	This is a 'belt and braces' additional paragraph to ensure the SRA is promptly informed of all matters necessary to its supervision and enforcement role.	• As above
7.9	"You do not subject any *person* to detrimental treatment for making or proposing to make a report or providing or proposing to provide information based on a reasonably held belief under paragraph 7.7 or 7.8 above, or paragraph 3.9, 3.10, 9.1(d) or (e) or 9.2(b) or (c) of the SRA Code of Conduct for Firms, irrespective of whether the *SRA* or another approved regulator subsequently	The reporting and notification duties are challenging and might place individuals in difficult positions. However, such reporting is a necessary function if the collective reputation of the profession is to be maintained and the SRA's status as an approved regulator is to be supported. This paragraph makes it clear that the regulator would regard it as unprofessional behaviour to treat an individual	• As above

continued on next page

Reference	Wording	Commentary	Compliance suggestions
	investigates or takes any action in relation to the facts or matters in question."	differently – in a detrimental way – where they have reasonable grounds for making this report. The reference to the SRA Code of Conduct for Firms does not apply to in-house counsel.	
7.10	"You act promptly to take any remedial action requested by the *SRA*. If requested to do so by the *SRA* you investigate whether there have been any serious breaches that should be reported to the *SRA*."	The SRA is entitled to ask in-house counsel to assist with remedial actions. This might include agreeing to implement a policy to support regulatory compliance or a supervision procedure etc.	• Ensuring that your non-solicitor employer understands the nature of your relationship with the SRA and their expectations of you
7.11	"You are honest and open with *clients* if things go wrong, and if a *client* suffers loss or harm as a result you put matters right (if possible) and explain fully and promptly what has happened and the likely impact. If requested to do so by the *SRA* you investigate whether anyone may have a claim against you, provide the	Don't forget that your client is the person or entity for whom you are providing legal services and whose position you are protecting or promoting as the case may be. In most in-house scenarios, the client will also be your employer, although this is not necessarily so. We are expected to acknowledge our mistakes, or other	• Training • Supervisory oversight of client matters • Procedure so that mistakes etc are raised within the legal team as quickly as possible

continued on next page

Reference	Wording	Commentary	Compliance suggestions
	SRA with a report on the outcome of your investigation, and notify relevant persons that they may have such a claim, accordingly."	matters that have gone awry, and be frank with our clients, making full and early disclosure to them.	
7.12	"Any obligation under this section or otherwise to notify, or provide information to, the *SRA* will be satisfied if you provide information to your firm's *COLP* or *COFA*, as and where appropriate, on the understanding that they will do so."	In private practice, authorised law firms must have a compliance officer for legal practice (COLP) and an officer for finance and administration (COFA), and this paragraph enables other employees to make reports to them on the understanding that they will deal with the SRA. There is no such requirement in connection with in-house practise, so all in-house solicitors have a personal duty to make the reports included in Chapter 7.	• Again, the employer must be made aware of personal reporting duties • Training • Informally, consider an internal procedure for the legal team so that reports are discussed with senior members

"Chapter 8 – When you are providing services to the public or a section of the public"

In-house counsel must determine whether this chapter is relevant to their employment. This chapter applies, and contains mandatory requirements, only in circumstances where a solicitor provides legal services to the public or a section of the public.

As in-house counsel you can provide legal services to your employer and other related bodies where there is some form of nexus or relationship such as is likely to be the case with companies within the same legal group. It is sensible for the legal team to understand the structure of the business and the relationships between all the entities within a group framework. These related parties are entitled to receive your legal services, subject of course to your initial consideration of regulatory and ethical issues such as your duty to act in each client's best interests, not to act in conflict situations etc.

Beyond this internal client base, in-house counsel can also provide certain legal services to external clients; that is, clients beyond the company family, and this is what is meant to be the reference in the chapter heading to the public or a section of the public.

This freedom was granted in 2019 with the introduction of the SRA Standards and Regulations. The STaRs abolished the previous long-standing regulatory restriction on in-house practice which had meant that in-house counsel had only been allowed to provide their services to the employer and a very tightly defined group of related bodies and most definitely not to members of the public. As there was not any statutory reason for this restriction, the SRA was obliged to remove this prohibition in 2019.

With this relaxation of regulatory restraints, in-house solicitors are now able to provide certain legal services to members of the public and the restrictions imposed on them are only those imposed in law. This means, for example, that because of the law,[6] in-house counsel cannot

6   The Legal Services Act 2007, section 12.

provide reserved legal activities to the public as this is restricted by the Legal Services Act to authorised or licensed business. Similarly, there are restrictions on other types of services, so that:

- In-house counsel cannot provide immigration services to members of the public unless their employer is authorised by the Office of the Immigration Services Commissioner.
- In-house counsel cannot provide claims management services to members of the public unless their employer is authorised for these services by the Financial Conduct Authority (FCA).
- In-house counsel cannot provide financial services to members of the public unless their employer is separately authorised for these services by the FCA.

The change in 2019 means that there is scope to provide certain legal services to members of the public while being employed in an in-house position. General legal advice seems the most obvious type of service. However, this freedom is not without risk, both for the client and for in-house counsel. In Chapter XII, we consider this, and the decisions associated with acting for members of the public, in more detail.

Briefly, in-house counsel should understand that they have no regulatory duty to accept all instructions, and they are well-advised to consider their own position before agreeing to instructions to act for a member of the public. Equally, clients receiving such services must understand that what they are not obtaining is the services of a solicitor who is in the same position as a lawyer providing those services from within private practice. The requirements of Chapter 8 of the SRA Code are designed to manage the risks of this relationship and to ensure that the client is protected and is not surprised by service standards, costs or other matters connected with their instructions.

In-house counsel should protect their own position and ensure that the protocol for accepting such instructions is well understood by the legal team and the employer, and that an audit trail is created which offers protection from regulatory and other criticisms. For in-house counsel who have experience of private practice client protocol, these paragraphs will seem very familiar.

Table 9: Compliance considerations and strategies

Reference	Wording	Commentary	Compliance suggestions
8.1	"You identify who you are acting for in relation to any matter."	It is important to be clear about the SRA's meaning when identification is mentioned in this paragraph. It is designed to manage and minimise the risk of being used for fraudulent purposes by requiring you to be satisfied that you have identified the client. The need to prove identity makes it harder for a fraudster to access legal services. However (and in contrast to identification and verification stipulated in the Money Laundering Regulations), the paragraph does not include prescriptive requirements and how identification is established is a judgement call for the solicitor.	• Inception process for use when acting for members of the public, which contains an identification procedure with provisions to refuse instructions if identity cannot be established • Training of relevant colleagues

continued on next page

Reference	Wording	Commentary	Compliance suggestions
8.2	"You ensure that, as appropriate in the circumstances, you either establish and maintain, or participate in, a procedure for handling complaints in relation to the legal services you provide."	The SRA does not currently provide us with a definition of complaint but previously this has been defined in the following way: "an oral or written expression of dissatisfaction which alleges that the complainant has suffered (or may suffer) financial loss, distress, inconvenience or other detriment",[i] and there seems no reason why we should not continue to use this meaning.	• Complaints handling procedure • Training
8.3	"You ensure that *clients* are informed in writing at the time of engagement about: (a) their right to complain to you about your services and your charges; (b) how a complaint can be made and to whom; and (c) any right they have to make a complaint to the *Legal Ombudsman* and when they can make any such complaint."	Clients must be notified about your Complaints Handling Procedure at the beginning of the matter. This information must be provided in writing and contain all the information listed in the paragraph.	• Client engagement letter/terms of business which contain this information • Training, including awareness training on the role and powers of the Ombudsman

continued on next page

Reference	Wording	Commentary	Compliance suggestions
8.4	"You ensure that when *clients* have made a complaint to you, if this has not been resolved to the *client's* satisfaction within 8 weeks following the making of a complaint they are informed, in writing: (a) of any right they have to complain to the *Legal Ombudsman*, the time frame for doing so and full details of how to contact the *Legal Ombudsman*; and (b) if a complaint has been brought and your complaints procedure has been exhausted: (i) that you cannot settle the complaint; (ii) of the name and website address of an alternative dispute resolution (ADR) approved body which would be competent to deal with the complaint; and (iii) whether you agree to use the scheme operated by that body."	This is described as the signposting paragraph. If your first tier Complaints Handling Procedure does not resolve a complaint within eight weeks, the client must be notified in writing of their right to refer the matter to the Legal Ombudsman (LeO). You are also obliged to tell the client whether you are prepared to refer the matter by way of ADR. Don't forget the requirements about cooperation and accountability in Chapter 7 of the Code. These behaviours apply to your relationship with LeO.	• Complaints handling template letter for use after eight weeks • Training

continued on next page

Reference	Wording	Commentary	Compliance suggestions
8.5	"You ensure that complaints are dealt with promptly, fairly, and free of charge."	It should be noted that the SRA has taken enforcement action against solicitors who have charged for the investigation of complaints.	• System to ensure that these requirements are met. This might include having a dedicated complaints handler who is trained on SRA and LeO expectations
8.6	"You give *clients* information in a way they can understand. You ensure they are in a position to make informed decisions about the services they need, how their matter will be handled and the options available to them."	It is important to remember that we act as our client's agent when protecting or promoting their interests. This requires us to obtain instructions which in turn is dependent on the client being given information from us in an appropriate way so that they understand what we can do, and their options so that they can make informed decisions.	• Consideration should be given to training on effective communication and other soft skills • Attendance notes or similar should be used to document client instructions
8.7	"You ensure that *clients* receive the best possible information about how their matter will be priced and, both at the time of engagement and when appropriate as their matter	Costs include fees and disbursements, and the objective of this paragraph is that clients are given realistic information about costs in order to make informed decisions about	• Client care information which records the costs, with a system for ongoing monitoring • Training

continued on next page

Reference	Wording	Commentary	Compliance suggestions
	progresses, about the likely overall cost of the matter and any *costs* incurred."	their next steps. Where it is not possible to provide a specific amount, then bear in mind that any estimate must be reasonably accurate and must be kept under review and changed as necessary with an explanation about the reason for any uplift. Any surprises, or excessively inaccurate estimates, are likely to be criticised by LeO which might also refer the matter to the SRA as unprofessional conduct.	
8.8	"You ensure that any *publicity* in relation to your practice is accurate and not misleading, including that relating to your charges and the circumstances in which *interest* is payable by or to *clients*."	Publicity is defined as follows: "all promotionalmaterial and activity, including the name or description of your firm, stationery, advertisements, brochures, websites, directory entries, media appearances, promotional press releases, and direct approaches to potential clients and other persons,	• Training

continued on next page

Reference	Wording	Commentary	Compliance suggestions
		whether conducted in person, in writing, or in electronic form, but does not include press releases prepared on behalf of a client".[ii]	
8.9	"You do not make unsolicited approaches to members of the public, with the exception of current or former *clients*, in order to advertise legal services provided by you, or your business or employer."	This is a ban on cold calling. It applies to in-house counsel and also anyone who might perform marketing and publicity services for the legal team.	• Training • Where marketing is performed by third parties (including other parts of the business), training of them plus spot checks of introduced clients
8.10	"You ensure that *clients* understand whether and how the services you provide are regulated. This includes: (a) explaining which activities will be carried out by you, as an *authorised person*; (b) explaining which services provided by you, your business or employer, and any *separate business* are regulated by an *approved regulator*; and	It is important that clients understand that while you are a regulated individual, subject to the STaRs and SRA oversight, your employer is not authorised by the SRA. The SRA has issued a guidance note to assist with this, such is the need to consider and protect the interests of members of the public and ensure that regulatory protections are understood.[iii]	• Template client care

continued on next page

Reference	Wording	Commentary	Compliance suggestions
	(c) ensuring that you do not represent any business or employer which is not authorised by the *SRA*, including any *separate business*, as being regulated by the *SRA*."		
8.11	"You ensure that *clients* understand the regulatory protections available to them."	This develops the information provisions in paragraph 8.10 of the Code. The client must be informed that the client understands that you do not have professional indemnity insurance as you are not providing services through an authorised business; whether you have alternative indemnity cover and the scope of this; and the fact that the client cannot make a claim on the SRA Compensation Fund.	• Client engagement letter/terms of business which contain this information • Training • Taking steps to remedy any misunderstandings that the client might harbour

[i] SRA Handbook Glossary, www.sra.org.uk.
[ii] SRA Glossary, www.sra.org.uk/solicitors/standards-regulations/glossary/.
[iii] SRA Guidance, 'Unregulated organisations giving information to clients', www.sra.org.uk/solicitors/guidance/unregulated-organisations-giving-information-clients/.

Chapter VI:

Sources of ethical knowledge for in-house counsel (3)

Other sections of the SRA Standards and Regulations

As a regulated individual, it is necessary to comply with all parts of the STaRs which are relevant to you. This means it is necessary to review the content and decide which sections apply to you and your circumstances, and then to decide not only how you will comply but also how you will demonstrate this compliance in practice.

The Principles and the SRA Code of Conduct for Solicitors, RELs and RFLs apply to all solicitors, regardless of form of practice, as these itemise the fundamental and individual ethical and regulatory duties.

The other parts of the STaRs are described below with a commentary about their relevance to the in-house community. The relevance should be considered and either discounted or steps taken to ensure compliance. Having a documented audit trail to demonstrate that this exercise has been undertaken might well prove useful should the SRA challenge any decisions made about application.

STaRs content which is relevant to all solicitors including in-house counsel

In addition to the Principles and the SRA Code of Conduct for Solicitors, RELS and RFLS, in-house counsel must take note of the following sections:

- Application, Notice, Review and Appeal Rules – these rules provide for our regulatory relationship with the SRA, with an explanation of the SRA's powers in respect of notices and our right in respect of applications, and with a framework for the review and appeals of decisions. These Rules should be noted in the context of regulatory communications, applications etc.

- Assessment of Character and Suitability Rules – these apply to individuals seeking admission or restoration to the roll of solicitors. These applications entitle the regulator to assess character and suitability traits and to make public interest decisions about eligibility and practising rights.

- Authorisation of Individuals Regulations – these apply in connection with the authorisation of individual solicitors and explain admission criteria, practising rights, conditions of authorisation and the circumstances in which the SRA can revoke authorisation.

- Overseas and Cross-border Practice Rules – for in-house counsel practising overseas, these Rules may replace the SRA Principles and the SRA Code of Conduct for Solicitors, RELs and RFLs with Overseas Principles. These are designed to appropriately and proportionately protect the reputation of the profession in the overseas context. It should be noted that these will undoubtedly be reviewed and updated as necessary to deal with the European Union position and anyone needing to comply must keep updated about any changes to these Rules. These Rules are described more fully in Chapter XI.

- Regulatory and Disciplinary Procedure Rules – apply to all regulated individuals, and the SRA itself, and describe how the latter will investigate and take disciplinary and regulatory action.
- Roll, Registers and Publication Regulations – describe the registers and roll maintained by the SRA.
- Glossary – certain of the SRA regulatory language has defined meaning for use in the STaRs toolkit.

STaRs content which is relevant to in-house counsel but only in certain circumstances

Adherence to certain parts of the regulatory toolkit is triggered by what you do and apply in these circumstances regardless of whether you are employed in private or in-house practice.

It is essential to make a judgement about whether the following sections are relevant to your practice:

- SRA Education, Training and Assessment Provider Regulations – in-house counsel are entitled to offer training to trainee solicitors subject to compliance with these Regulations and only if they become an authorised training provider.
- Transparency Rules – these apply only if in-house counsel provides legal services to the public or a section of the public (in accordance with Chapter 8 of the SRA Code of Conduct for Solicitors, RELs and RFLs) and in the following circumstances: (1) if you provide certain services to individuals or businesses you must publish information about costs and service provision (2) if you have a website, this must contain complaints handling information. It should be noted that the SRA is undertaking supervisory work in this area simply by checking websites etc. If these Rules apply to your practice, it would be prudent to have discussions with your web designers and IT colleagues to ensure that the need for compliance is understood.[1]

---

1 SRA News release, 21 January 2021, 'More firms sanctioned in transparency rules clampdown', www.sra.org.uk/sra/news/press/transparency-enforcement-starts/.

"Adherence to certain parts of the regulatory toolkit is triggered by what you do and apply in these circumstances regardless of whether you are employed in private or in-house practice."

- The Prescribed organisations and terms under which Solicitors, RELs and RFLs are allowed to hold client money in their own name – this regulatory statement is included within the STaRs and is addressed to in-house practitioners. There are strict limitations on the types of businesses or other entities in which in-house lawyers can hold client money in their own name; broadly, only solicitors employed by non-commercial bodies are entitled to hold client money in this way. A non-commercial body is defined in the Legal Services Act 2007 as a not-for-profit body, a community interest group or an independent trade union. These are the prescribed organisations for the purposes of this statement which explains the terms on which client money must be held. This is likely to be relevant to in-house counsel employed in non-prescribed organisations plus in-house counsel when volunteering and offering *pro bono* services from within these organisations.
- The prescribed circumstances in which you can withdraw client money from client account to pay to a charity of your choice – this statement only applies to solicitors employed in non-commercial bodies (see above) and who are holding client money in their own name. It provides regulatory direction about the circumstances in which client money can be withdrawn from client account when the funds cannot be returned to the client or the third-party payer.
- SRA Indemnity Rules 2012 – more experienced lawyers will recall that for many years professional indemnity insurance was provided to all private practitioners through a mutual fund known as the Solicitors Indemnity Fund (SIF). The SIF was wound up in 2000 and is currently providing run-off cover to members of private practices that were wound up before 31 August 2000 in certain circumstances. This fact is relevant to in-house counsel who might, because of previous work circumstances, rely on this run-off cover for any claims that arise. It is also important to note that SIF will close at some point and anyone who is affected by this will need to consider other indemnity options to protect their position.

STaRs content which is relevant to private practice only

The SRA does not only have a regulatory relationship with individual lawyers. As an approved regulator, the SRA has licensing powers and can authorise firms to provide legal services.

The following parts of the STaRs apply to these private practice entities, and therefore are not applied to in-house practice where the employer is not itself an authorised entity. These sections can be disregarded by in-house counsel unless they decide to form an authorised entity such as might be the case because they want to provide reserved legal services to a wider client base than is permitted as an employed individual. These are described as Alternative Business Structures (ABSs) and are described in more detail in Chapter XII. The sections are as follows:

- SRA Code of Conduct for Firms – the regulatory and ethical behaviours, and business controls, which are expected of authorised law firms and all employees (including non-qualified and business support staff).
- SRA Accounts Rules – very unlikely to apply to in-house practice on the basis that very few in-house counsel are allowed to hold client money.
- Authorisation of Firms Rules – the SRA's arrangements for authorising law firms.
- Financial Services (Scope) Rules and Financial Services (Conduct of Business) Rules – apply only to authorised firms and only in respect of the limited financial services which they are statutorily entitled to provide to their clients. In-house counsel wishing to provide financial services as part of their employment must consider their own, and their employer's position, under the Financial Services and Markets Act 2000.
- Indemnity (Enactment) Rules 2012, Indemnity Rules 2012 and Indemnity Insurance Rules – it is a condition of authorised status, that law firms hold professional indemnity insurance on prescribed terms. This mandatory requirement does not apply to in-house counsel.

- Compensation Fund Rules – these Rules apply to the operation of the SRA Compensation Fund. These apply largely to private practice, although grants can be made where the defaulting solicitor practises in a non-commercial body (ie, a not-for-profit body, a community interest company or an independent trade union). It should be noted that notwithstanding the disapplication of these Rules to the majority of in-house practitioners, all solicitors (with the exception of individuals employed as Crown Prosecutors) must contribute to the maintenance of the Compensation Fund.
- Statutory Trust Rules – in the event that a practice is subject to regulatory intervention, and therefore is closed by the SRA, these Rules contain the formula for how client money recovered from the firm is treated.

Nine essential ethical points about the STaRs which in-house counsel must understand

1. Understand the SRA Principles as they apply to both professional and personal behaviour.
2. First and foremost, you are a lawyer and an officer of the court with a duty to uphold the rule of law.
3. You must refuse to act on instructions which place you in a position where your professionalism is compromised.
4. Your professionalism will be scrutinised not only in respect of the services you provide to your client, but also in your relationships with colleagues, third parties and the court.
5. Your duty to encourage equality, diversity and inclusivity extends beyond simple compliance with the law.
6. Nothing or no one should compromise your independence and your delivery of good quality and ethically based services.
7. There is merit in adopting private practice style client etiquette.
8. Conflicts of interest are more common than you might imagine.
9. It is acceptable, and sometimes essential, to say no, whomever is asking.

Table 10: Myths about ethics and in-house practice

	The myth	The truth
1	The SRA focuses its supervisory and enforcement work on private practice and is not interested in in-house practice	The SRA is the approved regulator of all solicitors, Registered European Lawyers and Registered Foreign Lawyers regardless of where they work or the services which they provide. It will apply supervisory and enforcement powers to any scenario where it considers that its risk-based regulatory objectives are compromised and that includes in respect of in-house legal services provision and in respect of the professional or personal behaviour of in-house counsel.
2	In-house ethics can be moulded by employment requirements	It depends. The STaRs list a number of ethical behaviours that must be displayed. How they are displayed, and the means by which compliance is demonstrated, is usually not prescribed. This enables all practitioners to develop their own ways in which to ensure ethical duties are fulfilled. For example, there is an ethical duty not to provide legal services to a client in circumstances where an own interest conflict is identified. Some organisations (private law firms and non-law firm organisations) codify this with declaration of interest registers and policies whereas other entities choose to deliver training on the prohibition and then ask colleagues to make a personal judgement call on each new instruction. For in-house counsel, the starting point must be to assess the compatibility of internal procedures with their personal ethical duties and adopt those which are aligned, but add to those which do not deal with all ethical duties regulated by the SRA. The SRA expects to see such consideration and adaptations as are necessary.

continued on next page

	The myth	The truth
3	The SRA takes into account and accommodates the tensions that might arise between compliance with the STaRs and employment duties	The SRA understands that there might be tensions but would not find employment duties to be a reasonable excuse for not complying with the STaRs. In other words, the expectation is that in-house counsel will challenge inappropriate employment expectations and always adhere to ethical standards.
4	In-house counsel can disregard ethical duties which apply to service standards and client care behaviours	It is not true that in-house counsel can disregard client care ethical duties, or even client care conventions. Six-minute billing protocols might not be necessary, but the STaRs still require solicitors to consider their competence to deliver legal services, to consider whether instructions are appropriate and whether legal service provision is being effectively supervised and managed. It would be risky to abandon all client care and file management techniques simply because the client is an employee of the same business as counsel.
5	In-house counsel never have to consider conflicts of interests	Simply not true. The SRA and ethics identify two types of conflict (ie, own interest and client conflict) and expect us to manage both. A client conflict must be considered whenever you are asked to act for more than one party, notwithstanding your employment relationship or what you might be told about the instructions. Don't forget conflict assessment requires considering the vulnerability of the respective parties, and corporate entities can be as vulnerable in some circumstances as individuals seeking legal services.

continued on next page

	The myth	The truth
6	An undertaking given by in-house counsel is not binding on them personally	In-house counsel can give an undertaking, but they are, of course, professionally bound to comply with the terms, regardless of their client's instructions or position. This can sometimes place the individual in a more precarious position in terms of ability to honour the undertaking than would be the case in private practice where the owners of the business are likely also to be bound to honour the terms of an undertaking provided by a work colleague.
7	Because the SRA has no influence over the employer, there is no expectation that in-house counsel's ethical duties will extend to others in the business	Yes and no. The SRA has no influence, or regulatory reach as it is sometimes described, over non-solicitors in an unauthorised business. It is expected, however, that in-house counsel will seek to influence the behaviour of those that they work with. This is an aspirational expectation and the SRA hopes that in-house counsel with more seniority and a greater sphere of influence will be proportionately more ethically pervasive in the business than might be possible for junior counsel. Where in-house counsel head up legal teams, it is expected that their personal duties and accountability in respect of supervision and management will influence the ethical culture of the team.

Chapter VII :

Agreeing responsibilities – the pinch points

Businesses employ in-house counsel for a diverse number of reasons including, to be blunt, sometimes simply for the reason that there has always been a lawyer even though no one is quite sure why, or even know what they can or what they should ask the lawyer to do!

It should go without saying that solicitors employed in-house must ensure that necessary conversations take place about the services which they can perform, and more importantly, what they will not be able to do.

Obviously, this requires a discussion about the solicitor's competence which might be a surprise to the employer but nevertheless is an important point to be discussed. We have already discussed the fact that solicitors are granted an annual licence to practise, and this practising certificate is not (except in the case of advocacy rights) issued with any

"It should go without saying that solicitors employed in-house must ensure that necessary conversations take place about the services which they can perform, and more importantly, what they will not be able to do."

qualifications. This is both a good and bad thing; it means that there are no restrictions on your ability – other than personal self-restraint and knowing your strengths and weaknesses – to practise in any area of law. The downside is that this freedom means that self-control must be exercised.

Competency duties require you to say no to instructions which stretch you beyond your knowledge capabilities; to act in such circumstances is likely to create difficulties with compliance and with the principle that you must act in the best interests of each client (SRA Principle 7). In other words, a solicitor who tries to be a 'jack of all trades', or an employer who considers that in-house counsel should be able to turn their hand to any type of legal services, needs to consider the implications for themselves and for the business.

Ethical duties would also require you to refuse to act on instructions in certain circumstances. Not having time or appropriate resources to deliver a proper standard of service is envisaged by the duties in Chapter 3 of the SRA Code of Conduct for Solicitors, RELs and RFLs. Identify conflicts – own interest, client conflicts and conflicts of confidentiality and disclosure duties – as described in Chapter 6 of the Code, is another source of reasons to refuse to act.

There are remedies to misunderstandings about what you can and cannot do. Firstly, a job description which clearly contains the agreed legal services which will be provided by in-house counsel is recommended. This requires conversations and agreement at an early stage of the employment relationship about the need for you to be able to say no to some instructions. Secondly, the business's agreement about the alternative means of acquiring legal support which go beyond in-house counsel's competence, and the ongoing role that will be expected, should also be obtained.

Outsourcing as a means of receiving legal services

Outsourcing to fill the gaps is commonplace, and while others in the business might be involved in the mechanics of this operation such as budget and procurement, in-house counsel has a professional role and responsibilities for managing the relationship with external lawyers.

The STaRs are silent on this specific point, and there is no specific paragraph in the SRA Code of Conduct for Solicitors, RELs and RFLs which addresses the subject of outsourcing. This is a change from the previous regulatory toolkit (the SRA Handbook) which did deal with the subject as follows:

- *You do not outsource reserved legal activities to a person who is not authorised to conduct such activities*
- *… Where you outsource legal activities or any operational functions that are critical to the delivery of any legal activities, you ensure such outsourcing:*

    (a) Does not adversely affect your ability to comply with, or the SRA's ability to monitor your compliance with, your obligations in the Handbook;

    (b) Is subject to contractual arrangements that enable the SRA or its agents to obtain information from, inspect the records (including electronic records) of, or enter the premises of, the third party, in relation to the outsourced activities or functions;

    (c) Does not alter your obligations towards your clients; and

    (d) Does not cause you to breach the conditions with which you must comply in order to be authorised and to remain so.[1]

The absence of a like-for-like paragraph in the STaRs does not detract from regulatory and ethical expectations and obligations to manage this relationship. The effectiveness and suitability of the outsourcing arrangement requires input and oversight from in-house counsel. After all, in-house counsel is better equipped to sense test what is happening in these circumstances. Notwithstanding the source of the legal advice, the client is entitled to receive assurances from in-house counsel that their best interests are being protected.

---

1 SRA Handbook, SRA Code of Conduct 2011, outcomes (7.9) and (7.10), www.sra.org.uk/solicitors/handbook/.

In-house counsel will want to consider the following topics when managing outsourcing relationships:

- Is there internal agreement as to what services will be outsourced?
- Is there an understanding that outsourcing might be necessary if in-house counsel has a conflict of interests or a conflict between duties of confidentiality and disclosure (as described in Chapter 6 of the SRA Code of Conduct for Solicitors, RELs and RFLs)?
- Does in-house counsel have the authority to instruct external legal advisers?
- If the business has panel firms, is in-house counsel involved in the tender process and is there a mechanism for maintaining appropriate due diligence checks on the panel firms?
- Does in-house counsel properly scope the instructions so that the external legal advisers are clear about their retainer?
- Are fees and disbursements clear?
- Is there appropriate means to quality control the service received?

THOUGHT LEADERSHIP

Rebecca Atkinson is the director of risk and compliance at Howard Kennedy LLP, and has reviewed countless agreements where outsourced services are being sought by in-house counsel. She provides us with her top tips for ensuring the success of this relationship from the perspective of the firm to whom services are outsourced.

Top tips when outsourcing to external legal advisers/counsel

When instructing external advisers, it is vital to get the relationship on the right setting from the get-go. This will not only ensure the smooth running of the matter but will also prevent any disagreements down the line.

Below are some tips to ensuring both sides, in-house counsel as client and the external adviser, understand what needs to be done and how the work should be conducted.

- *Decide who will be the lead contact at your business* – deciding who the lead contact at your business is for the matter, communicating this to the external adviser and confirming if any others in your business will be providing instructions may prevent confusion or issues occurring in the future. You would also do well to ensure that you have a client relationship partner or equivalent to go to should you have any concerns.
- *Be clear about the scope of the work* – this needs to be set out in a sufficiently detailed way in the external adviser's engagement letter. Be sure to check what is in and out of scope. If something is considered to be out of scope in the letter and you want it in scope, raise it from the outset. It goes without saying that you need to make sure you receive an engagement letter from external advisers.
- *Be clear about the cost* – this needs to be considered and documented in the external adviser's engagement letter and if not, in a separate document. Consider whether a cap should be put in place or an agreement to be notified when costs reach a certain level before further work is conducted.
- *Be clear about what you will accept to be billed and not* – some external advisers will want to charge for photocopying, taxis or research on matters that you would not expect the external adviser to charge for. Consider the external advisers' terms and conditions carefully for these items.
- *Consider how often you expect to be billed, on what payment terms and how* – external advisers may want to bill monthly or on an *ad hoc* basis. Consider whether this is right for you and your business. Further consider when you will agree to pay, ie, 30 days after delivery of the invoice or later. External advisers

are likely to place on their bill that it is payable immediately, but this might not be feasible for your business. Lastly consider if you want to engage a third-party supplier for the external adviser to place their invoices through. There are platforms which can form part of the invoicing process and collate data on what the spend is and for what type of work. For large pieces of work such as litigation, this can prove a useful way of keeping your eye on the spend.

- *Consider your business's stance on conflicts* – if you are instructing a solicitor in England and Wales, they will be bound by the SRA Codes of Conduct which provides great comfort. However, your business might want to consider coming to an agreement about the external adviser acting for a competitor business which, while it might not technically cause a Code of Conduct conflict, might cause your business some ethical unease. If you are instructing overseas legal advisers, check their terms to ensure that you are not being asked to give a blanket waiver to all possible future conflicts.

- *Check the adviser's terms of business* – there are of course many good reasons why you should do this and here are some of them:

  - Check you are happy with the limitation of liability provided and whether it is enough. Consider asking for more if necessary. Remember solicitors' firms in England and Wales must provide the minimum cover of £3 million. You should seek a limitation that would cover the value of any negligence on the legal adviser's part. To think of this, you need to catastrophise a bit.

  - Check you are happy with the file destruction policy.

  - Check you are happy with any indication that the external adviser will inform third parties that they act for you on marketing material or to rankings agencies.

- Check you are happy with the termination clauses, resolution clauses and applicable law.
- *Consider asking the external adviser to accept the engagement on your terms of business* – you may decide that in fact you would prefer that the external adviser acts on your terms. This has many advantages for businesses as naturally those terms will capture all the areas of concern for your business. It will not, however, contain all the information that legal advisers are obliged under their own regulatory regime to impart, and therefore the external adviser may need to suggest amendments. A compromise would be for the external adviser to accept your terms if you agree to accept theirs where there is no competing contradictory clause. An example would be the external adviser's complaints procedure which they are obliged to inform clients of at the beginning of a matter.
- *Keep the dialogue open* – lastly, make sure there is good open dialogue between you and the external adviser. Emails can be misread and misinterpreted. Although it is always best to document instructions and agreements, sometimes speaking on the telephone is better and maybe even better than that, video call.

The jack of all trades misunderstandings

Developing the twin themes of misunderstandings about competency and the reality of what an in-house counsel is employed to do, there is the need to be crystal clear about risk management of compliance with the law. We have already briefly referred to the risk associated with an employer believing that in-house counsel can turn their legal hand to any legal topic, however tenuous the connection with the terms of the individual's employment contract.

A case in point is the need to be clear about responsibilities where the business must comply with legislation or face legal (and of course reputational) consequences. Topics that spring to mind include data protection, tax evasion legislation, equality, modern slavery, employment and health and safety legislation. The topic base is endless.

It is true that in-house counsel have personal duties to "keep up to date with and follow the law and regulation governing the way you work" (SRA Code of Conduct for Solicitors, RELS and RFLs, paragraph 7.1). There is also the duty to ensure that others whom they manage "are competent to carry out their role, and keep their professional knowledge and skills, as well as understanding of their legal, ethical and regulatory obligations, up to date" (paragraph 3.6).

However, nothing in these paragraphs conveys an assumption or an obligation that in-house counsel will be responsible for ensuring compliance with all legislation of relevance to the business. This might be an easy, even lazy, assumption for the business to make. It is essential that in-house counsel clearly identify who is responsible for what, and that there are established roles and, more importantly, hand-off points between these roles.

An example – data protection

Data protection springs to mind. Business considerations stretch to a number of issues: compliance with the UK General Data Protection Regulation and other data protection law; sometimes data protection laws globally; the relationship with the Information Commissioner's Office and, if necessary, their international counterparts; the publishing and upkeep of privacy notices; other policies, controls and procedures to manage risks; consideration of marketing practices; information security systems; data subject matters and data breach risk management.

No one underestimates the enormity of the subject or the complexity of the governance of the risk. While the risk should be managed, nowhere is it prescribed that lawyers and the in-house legal team must be responsible for compliance with data protection law and data management in practice.

Larger businesses often employ a risk and governance team, and they usually take the lead with management of this risk. It is important to establish what they and the business expect of in-house counsel; is it to not interfere in their areas of expertise, or is it to keep them updated in changes in the law, or to review policies or something else? Any of these answers can be correct but it is important that the role is clearly understood.

In smaller businesses, where there is no such governance department, perhaps there is only one legally trained individual (ie, you in your role as in-house counsel). This triggers the need for discussions to establish and protect your position. For example, is there an assumption that you will take responsibility for managing the topic? If this is the case, are you competent (in terms of both knowledge, seniority and resources) to lead the business's response? Perhaps it's the case that there is no clear home for this, and everyone thinks that someone else is taking the lead? What would happen in the event of a data security issue and how quickly would you be explaining your role?

Data protection management cannot be left to chance and in-house counsel should ensure that responsibilities are agreed and that their role is exact and well understood.

Every business should agree the areas of legislation which must be understood. Other legislation which is likely to be relevant in the businesses which employ in-house counsel include legislation arising in respect of equality matters, anti-bribery and corruption, tax evasion, modern slavery issues, money laundering, financial services, advertising, health and safety laws etc.

In-house counsel must be clear as to the chain of command for management of the risk of breaking the law and the business's expectations of them. Bear in mind that the SRA is a risk-based regulator, and much of its supervisory and enforcement work starts because of concerns about behaviours or events which are detrimental or damaging to the profession's collective reputation. The SRA does act on adverse media stories. While a legal offence committed by a business is of no interest to the SRA, in-house counsel's role might well concern them and trigger regulatory conversations. Having proof that ownership of legal risk management has been discussed and agreed will be useful evidence to share with the regulator in such circumstances.

Top tips for managing the business's expectations

✔ Have an agreed job description which clearly delineates your responsibilities, so that your competencies are understood and there are other agreed options to provide services which you cannot perform.

✔ Have a clearly agreed role in outsourcing of legal services to external lawyers.

✔ Identify areas of legal compliance which must be managed by the business and ensure that there is understanding of in-house counsel's role.

✔ Ensure that where in-house counsel has responsibilities, they also have the knowledge, resources and seniority to be effective.

.

Chapter VIII:
Setting the tone (1)
The in-house counsel as team leader

In-house counsel who lead a legal team, or those who might lead others in providing particular legal services, face a number of challenges. Not only are they in senior roles as legal advisers with their own work commitments, but they also have wider responsibilities, both in respect of the delivery of legal services and also of a pastoral nature, in respect of the team they head up.

The equivalent in private practice are the partners, directors or LLP members who own the firm. As owners, they have clear duties to ensure that they display effective governance of their authorised business. The required compliance and business standards are described to them (in the SRA Authorisation of Firms Rules) and have regulatory weight which justifies the development of internal procedures, controls and policies.

"The SRA has an expectation that senior in-house counsel will influence the professionalism of their colleagues and create the frequently described, but rarely fully explained, compliance culture or ethos of their team which facilitates the delivery of good quality and ethically based legal services."

There is nothing similar that can be applied by in-house team leaders as a starting point or a justification for what might be necessary. The Authorisation of Firms Rules do not apply as the employing business is not authorised by the SRA, meaning the SRA can only look to the behaviours of the regulated individuals. The members of the team are not necessarily all solicitors. Some colleagues might be subject to regulation by other approved regulators such as the Bar Standards Board in the case of barrister colleagues, others might not be qualified legal practitioners but are fulfilling legal roles, others may work in a business support role.

In other words, an in-house team leader faces similar challenges to private practice managers, yet without the regulatory structural help or direction. Notwithstanding these facts, the SRA has an expectation that senior in-house counsel will influence the professionalism of their colleagues and create the frequently described, but rarely fully explained, compliance culture or ethos of their team which facilitates the delivery of good quality and ethically based legal services.

A team leader should be clear about the SRA's expectations of this role and develop compliance and business systems that are appropriate to manage the risks that come with lack of direction or purpose as might otherwise be the case. Such an exercise will facilitate an easier relationship with the SRA, particularly if challenged about behaviours. It can also be useful if the legal team is subject to an internal audit and needs evidence to address any risk and compliance concerns arising from that quarter.

THOUGHT LEADERSHIP

*To set the scene, the following contribution is from **Richard Macmillan** who is general counsel with Moorfields Eye Hospital NHS Foundation Trust. To illustrate the position of a senior in-house counsel, Richard has answered some questions about his role.*

Q: Can you provide a brief description of your career history, including when you were admitted, your specialisms and types of employment prior to joining Moorfields?

A. I was admitted in 2008 following completion of my training with Osborne Clarke in the City. I started my career as an employment specialist, primarily as a litigator. After a spell in the City, I focused my career on representing claimants and trade unions. I then moved in-house and joined the British Heart Foundation as an employment lawyer and gradually broadened my practise to include general commercial, data and intellectual property. I became Head of Legal before joining Moorfields.

Q: When did you join Moorfields?

A. I joined in September 2019.

Q: What type of services do you and your team deliver and to whom?

A. We provide a wide range of services across the entire trust following a business partnering model. Moorfields is pre-eminent in research and development in new treatments for Ophthalmology and so a significant amount of our work is focused on R&D, providing general commercial advice on major collaborations with organisations such as Google Health, as well as supporting the team on the exploitation of our intellectual property portfolio. We manage all litigation, from commercial disputes to employment tribunal claims, to clinical negligence. We also support our Information Governance team with data protection matters and support on all major projects including the exciting construction of the new hospital building, which will be an integrated research centre with University College London.

Q: What's the size and composition of your team (eg, how many legally qualified staff, how is the team sub-divided etc)?

A. We are a team consisting of two lawyers and admin staff. Both lawyers are Business Partners, covering all the main departments at the Trust, but external lawyers provide support.

Q: How do you see your team leader role?

A. My role is to provide strategic leadership for the legal team and to ensure that the Trust gets the focused legal advice that it requires. I am also there to support my team members, but to ensure they feel empowered to take the lead in key areas they are entrusted with.

Q: How do you ensure that there is evidence of compliance with SRA regulatory requirements and ethical behaviours?

A. I regularly supervise my team to ensure compliance with all regulatory matters and ethical behaviours. The team are free to use some of the legal budget to ensure they have the right professional development in place.

Q: Does the team have documented policies, controls and procedures?

A. We do around how we manage our case load in terms of case management and also the use of the legal budget for external spend.

Q: How are team members supported and/or monitored?

A. My team and I have a good working relationship and they are free to approach me at any time where they need support and guidance. I also have regular one-to-one meetings with all my team so that we can discuss current workload and any issues they might have. However, I consider it important to empower teams as I believe this leads to greater productivity if there is a sense of ownership over workload.

Q: **What is your view of the role of senior in-house counsel in terms of creating the right environment for ethical behaviour?**

A. General Counsel should be the 'conscience' of any organisation and be willing to speak as its moral compass to senior management and the board when difficult ethical issues are being discussed. This is partly because the perception of lawyers is that they are more objective and direct with advice whatever the circumstances, and so that voice is trusted. In turn, this helps create the right atmosphere for ethical behaviour by giving others the confidence to speak out without reprisal where they have concerns, as there is an example with the GC or other in-house counsel for all to see. It is not uncommon for me to be approached by colleagues to raise issues, knowing their concerns will be treated confidentially or raised at the appropriate level. This is particularly important in the health sector.

Q: **What are the challenges of being head of an in-house legal team?**

A. As with most supporting functions, justifying your value and contribution, given we are often a cost centre, is always the main challenge. This makes it challenging to get extra resources for your team, whether by way of people or budget. A challenge can be that lawyers are perceived as being unapproachable and therefore (somewhat unfairly) to be avoided! However, once you demonstrate value and support beyond that of a traditional lawyer, to be the trusted business adviser, real benefit can be seen. Establishing good working relationships (for example through a business partnering model) can really help with this so that the legal team can help facilitate wider business objectives. Another challenge is that lawyers are often brought in to advise at the last minute and at that point raising unexpected issues and/or concerns at the eleventh hour. Far better to be involved in major projects early on, so that you can raise points much earlier and shape advice according to risk.

Q: What advice would you give anyone who has been recently appointed as head of an in-house legal team?

A. The first piece of advice is to be a social butterfly with your new colleagues! Get to know key individuals (especially key decision makers) rather than waiting patiently in your office for instructions. Building good working relationships is key to a successful in-house team. From there I would always ensure you are in the right meetings, particularly key board and/or committee meetings. This is critical for profile raising and understanding the work of your organisation and its risk appetite, which in turn helps you finesse your legal advice so that it is commercial and risk based rather than being theoretical. Thirdly, if you are not just a sole in-house team, really get to know and understand the strengths of your team so that you can maximise its productivity and contribution. From there, you can develop a strategy for the future that is focused on the needs of your organisation. Even if you do not have a team, you can still think of a strategy for the future and convey the possibilities. This may be the first step to building a successful legal team for the future.

Q: How do you facilitate the effective use of your legal team by your internal clients?

A. Business Partnering is key. Where colleagues have that first point of contact, there is always someone to approach in order to guide them through all their legal requirements, including using external lawyers where necessary or by delegating to others within the team. The model also allows effective communication between the legal team and colleagues, so that we understand key issues early, hopefully preventing them from becoming bigger problems further down the line and thus draining more resource.

- -
Q: Do your clients understand the implications of working with regulated lawyers?
A. Yes, but given we all work within the health sector, the importance of regulation and adhering to high ethical standards is widely understood.

The starting point – effective governance

Establishing effective governance arrangements is an obvious starting point for in-house counsel who is in a position of seniority in terms of leading a team. An individual in this role is expected to be able to exert influence over others. This is more easily and effectively achieved through the creation of good order and, for this reason, it makes sense to use some of the infrastructure more readily recognised in private practice. It is advisable to have structures, arrangements, systems and other controls in place to support appropriate behaviour and consistency and to demonstrate to both the employer and SRA that the individual has contributed to a well-ordered environment through the creation of a suitable framework which supports the provision of good quality legal advice.

Given that this is not codified by the SRA, the type of framework is largely a matter of business choice. However, this should be designed to reflect the size of the team, the composition and their experience, the type of work delivered and the need to manage identified legal and ethical risks.

Sense-testing questions will include the following:

- How should the team be structured – should we compartmentalise different workstreams? Do we need an organisational chart for the team?
- Who are the team leaders? What is in their role description? Are they fit for purpose or do they need additional training or coaching?
- Do we need to designate other specific role holders – supervisors, individuals with specific equality and other responsibilities etc?

- Are expectations about individual responsibilities clearly defined? Are we confident that junior colleagues, non-solicitors and business support staff understand our expectations?
- What policies, controls and procedures should be drafted to ensure consistency of approach?
- More generally, what is needed in terms of personal development and other training?

Effective supervision

There simply cannot be an effective governance framework without the inclusion of a supervision infrastructure.

The business in which in-house counsel is employed will no doubt have its own expectations about lines of responsibility and reporting functions which are deemed necessary to ensure that corporate objectives are achieved. This is unlikely to be a complete answer or substitute for what the SRA expects to see in terms of supervision, and in-house counsel must consider whether an additional regime should be implemented within the legal team to meet their needs.

The SRA regards effective supervision as a means of influencing legal team members, whoever they may be, and bestows responsibilities on individual solicitors to ensure that this happens in practice.

Unfortunately, the SRA does not define words like supervisor, supervise, manager or manage for these purposes. In the absence of what would have been helpful and defining explanations and instructions, it is vital that this has been considered as part of the team structure building exercise. The team should be assembled with clearly owned responsibilities and include the identification of individuals who are responsible for both the supervision and management of other colleagues when they provide legal services.

This is because solicitors who supervise and/or manage others who are providing legal services are required to comply with individual duties in the SRA Code of Conduct for Solicitors, RELs and RFLS.

The relevant paragraphs are quoted below:

3.5 Where you supervise or manage others providing legal services:
   (a) you remain accountable for the work carried out through
      them; and
   (b) you effectively supervise work being done for clients.

3.6 You ensure that the individuals you manage are competent to carry
   out their role, and keep their professional knowledge and skills,
   as well as understanding of their legal, ethical and regulatory
   obligations, up to date.[1]

The language of these paragraphs is forceful, direct and, quite frankly, hostage-taking in regulatory terms. You are told that "you remain accountable" and that you must "effectively" supervise and "ensure" others are competent. In other words, this language is used to insist that a supervisor or other team leader be able to justify not only their own actions but also the actions of others and the relationship between them both. This type of double scrutiny does filter through to the considerations of the Solicitors Disciplinary Tribunal who will often discipline an individual for professional misconduct and also look more widely to see why this was allowed to happen. In other words, the SRA is entitled to ask a solicitor supervisor or manager about misconduct and how it was able to occur on that individual's watch.

The safe response should start with the creation of a structure chart which shows both the team and the internal client responsibilities, decision making and reporting lines. Aligned to this, the structure should be supported by a robust and documented supervision policy which demonstrates expectations of both supervisors and those who are supervised and provides certainty to all individuals. A policy which is workable in practice is also a useful means to demonstrate to the regulator that there is acknowledgement of the expectations in the SRA Code and a means to achieve the objectives.

---

1   SRA Code of Conduct for Solicitors, Registered European Lawyers and Registered Foreign Lawyers, www.sra.org.uk/solicitors/standards-regulations/code-conduct-solicitors/.

The content of any supervision policy will reflect the circumstances of the environment. It is unwise to use template or 'off the shelf' policies or the type that simply make the bold (and often untrue) statement that doors are always open and similar. Instead, a policy that reflects the needs of individuals within the team and has a clearly described methodology about how effective supervision will be achieved, is more likely to prove a useful resource.

Suggestions for the content of a supervision policy drafted to satisfy SRA requirements include:

- An explanation about the purpose of the policy. Ideally, the policy will be drafted in such a way as to support colleagues in providing good quality and ethically based legal services to clients, and to identify training and other needs and to facilitate appropriate solutions.

- Clarity about the role of the supervisor – an effective supervisor is one who has technical expertise, but also understands ethical skills, and is approachable, has mentorship qualities and can make decisions overlaid with a realism that the role is designed not only to support an individual but also to protect the business and clients.

- An explanation about what is expected of the individual who is supervised – a supervisory relationship will only work when there is openness and cooperation on both sides. The supervised individual needs to have confidence in the process to enable frank and timely conversations.

- Description of the types of events that demonstrate supervision – of course, this will be the one-to-one and similar performance-related meetings that the business no doubt has already implemented. In addition, file reviews and department meetings, access to supervisors at all times, mentoring and training support are all indicators of a supervision regime and should also be considered as ways of demonstrating effective supervision in practice.

Policies, controls and procedures

The larger the organisation, the larger the office manual will be, and in-house counsel will naturally be expected to comply with a myriad of business-wide policies, controls and procedures simply because they are employees.

This alone is unlikely to be sufficient to prove to the SRA that in-house counsel are also acting in compliance with regulatory and ethical duties as described in the SRA Standards and Regulations. In-house leaders will want to consider the merits of a team-specific office manual to cover these additional duties and to ensure that members of the team know what is expected of them.

To be clear, this does not mean that in-house counsel are able to disregard business-wide policies, but in order to tie up loose ends, they must consider whether additional policies are required to fill regulatory gaps.

This requires knowledge of the STaRs and the business's policies. A benchmarking exercise to show when the latter will support compliance with the former is suggested, including an explanation as to why this is believed to be the case, is sensible. Thereafter, it should be easier to identify gaps and draft additional team-specific policies to supplement what exists.

While the SRA rarely prescribes how regulatory compliance, and the maintenance of an ethical position, is achieved, it is undoubtedly the case that it expects to see compliance in practice with appropriate statements of policy, and procedures and systems rolled out to support this policy. It is also expected that these policies, controls and procedures will have been designed to suit the specific needs of the solicitors and their team rather than simply be standardised documents with less relevance to the specific circumstances. In other words, the larger the team, the larger the need for more detailed audit evidence, whereas lone in-house counsel will rarely require such a detailed response.

Some suggestions about the content of a legal team (sometimes described as risk and compliance) manual are shown in the table below which includes an explanation as to why these should be considered.

Table 11: Suggestions for a compliance manual

	Suggested policy	Commentary
1	Statement about the role of the team	An explanation about the legal provision and advisory role of the team sets the scene for members of the team and also internal clients who may be unclear as to the services which are available. A statement about the legal services the team will provide, together with a reminder about the services not provided, is useful.
2	Statement about the application of the policies and the overlap with requirements of non-SRA regulatory bodies	The manual will need to address both solicitors and non-solicitors in the team. Reference to the SRA and the Standards and Regulations should be made; it should be stated that ethical behaviours expected by this regulator are demonstrated by compliance with the manual. If other lawyers are regulated by different bodies (eg, the Bar Standards Board, CILEX etc) then the manual should be followed unless the requirements place the individuals in breach of their own regulatory duties. This is unlikely; all regulators are approved by the Legal Services Board and all must comply with the regulatory objectives in the Legal Services Act 2007. If anyone considers that they cannot comply with the procedures etc in the office manual for this reason, they must speak with the senior members of the team. Non-lawyers will be expected to comply with the manual and behave in an ethically compliant way.
3	Description of SRA Principles	The manual should recite the Principles. They apply to everyone in their professional lives and solicitors must note that the Principles also apply to them in their personal lives.
4	SRA Code of Conduct for Solicitors, RELs and RFLs	A brief description is appropriate; this is the solicitors' personal conduct Code.
5	Equality, diversity and inclusion policy	While the business undoubtedly will have its own equality policies, this manual should include reference to SRA requirements (SRA Principle 6 and SRA Code paragraph 1.1) and these duties should be described with an indication of behavioural expectations within the team.

continued on next page

	Suggested policy	Commentary
6	Undertakings policy	The manual should include the SRA's definition of an undertaking (STaRs Glossary) plus the requirement contained in SRA Code paragraph 1.3 and directions as to who is entitled to give an undertaking, how it is recorded etc.
7	Competency policy	To deal with learning and development, plus the need for solicitors to confirm competency on an annual basis during the practising certificate renewal exercise, this section should make reference to the Statement of Solicitor Competence and direction as to how training etc should be recorded by individuals.
8	Statement about job titles and other publicity	The 'solicitor' term is a protected title under the Solicitors Act 1974, and there are other restrictions relating to descriptions such as 'counsel' and 'lawyer'. Using a title erroneously or in a misleading way may give rise to regulatory and, possibly, criminal offences. A statement about the use of titles is prudent.
9	Supervision policy	In terms of supervision of legal services, the SRA places personal duties and accountability on the shoulders of solicitors. A well-designed supervision policy to explain how supervision will be effected is advisable, as is training for solicitors' supervisors to ensure that they understand their responsibilities.
10	Conflict policy	No doubt the business has expectations about personal interest conflicts and registers of appointments etc. This additional policy is needed to explain and deal with the SRA's requirements about own interest and conflict of interest situations as described in Chapter 6 of the SRA Code.
11	Confidentiality policy	Confidentiality and the duties owed to clients must be clearly expressed. Practical steps to manage confidentiality should be demonstrated, eg, reminders about safe storage of paper documents or restricted use of the business's IT system, behaviours when out of the office etc. Disclosure duties and the practical steps which are expected if confidentiality and disclosure behaviours cannot be reconciled is usefully added here.

continued on next page

	Suggested policy	Commentary
12	Social media policy	Bearing in mind the SRA's concerns about offensive communications, a policy to remind everyone of the need to consider the appropriateness of both professional and personal social media usage is advisable.
13	Outsourcing policy	The team is unlikely to be a 'one stop shop' for the provision of legal services, so a policy about the use of external legal advice is sensible. This should include a reminder about the continuing role of the team in supporting the internal client.
14	Client onboarding procedure	It is sensible to document who within the business is entitled to give the team instructions; what information is required; records which should be made about the scope of the instructions; how the file will be managed; the information which must be given to the client; who will be supervising the matter etc.
15	Client care procedures (including a complaints policy)	If the team provides legal services to members of the public in accordance with Chapter 8 of the SRA Code, additional procedures are required to deal with client identification duties, provision of information about the scope of the retainer, costs etc, terms of business, complaints handling policy and information etc.
16	Training policy	This adds to the information about competency and is a statement about training requirements and availability. Record-keeping requirements should also be added.
17	Whistleblowing policy	No doubt the business has a whistleblowing policy to report concerns connected with the business's objectives etc. This additional policy deals with the reporting of ethical or regulatory concerns.
18	Reporting and notification policy	All solicitors have a duty to self-report conduct and other issues, and matters arising in connection with their practice, and this should be signposted in a policy.
19	Risk management statement	Again, the business will have its own risk management strategies. If risks which might arise in the legal team are not included in this document, it is advisable to include these within the team's own manual with management and mitigation procedures added. In addition, the team should include some recognition of the relevance of risks identified by the SRA to their work and environment.

Risk management

The SRA is a risk-based regulator applying risk assessment to the individuals which it regulates (and, in private practice, also the firms which it authorises or licenses). Interest in our risk management response should be less of a surprise to in-house practitioners than it has been to their private practice colleagues. This is because in-house counsel are usually employed in businesses where risk management is a business interest and an accepted feature of the governance arrangements.

Risk management is a regulatory duty imposed on all private practitioners who are obliged, courtesy of the SRA Code of Conduct for Firms, to "identify, monitor and manage all materials risks" to their business.[2] There is nothing comparable for in-house practice, yet it is assumed that in-house counsel, as well as lawyers in law firms, will exercise risk management.

The SRA produces risk resources to aid our understanding of regulatory priorities. Most notably, the annually produced SRA Risk Outlook provides an insight into regulatory analysis of high-risk matters. The latest Outlook[3] prioritises the following topics: anti-money laundering; client money; diversity in the profession; information and cyber security; integrity and ethics; meeting legal needs and standards of service.

Obviously, not all of these identified risks are relevant to in-house practice. Nevertheless, it would be prudent for the in-house team leader to reflect on which of these categories of risks materialise in their surroundings and, if appropriate, add procedures to manage and minimise the impact. This might well be through a connection with business risk management policies or, if necessary, a separate statement to deal with issues that might uniquely arise within the legal team. In much the same way as it is suggested that a team manual is worked up to fill gaps left due to their omission from the business's systems,

---

2 SRA Code of Conduct for Firms, paragraph 2.5, www.sra.org.uk/solicitors/standards-regulations/code-conduct-firms.

3 SRA Risk Outlook 2020/2021, www.sra.org.uk/risk/outlook/risk-outlook-2020-21/.

in-house counsel are well advised to consider the SRA's risk appetite and demonstrate which of the current risks are present in their team, and if so, the management and mitigation techniques, and also add other risks that are relevant because of their circumstances.

Record-keeping

In private practice, the owners of authorised entities are given the mandatory regulatory duty to "keep and maintain records to demonstrate compliance with your obligations under the SRA's regulatory arrangements".[4] Of course, no such duty can be imposed on in-house team leaders. However, the SRA does speak to individual solicitors regardless of where they practise and says that you must be "able to justify your decisions and actions in order to demonstrate compliance with your obligations under the SRA's regulatory arrangements".[5]

Being expected to justify a decision to the SRA is another example of use of words which add weight to the regulatory position. If asked to justify something, you will be expected to show the SRA your thinking or prove that you were right in your analysis and a decision or action was reasonable. Experience of enforcement work shows that it is easier to be able to justify yourself with contemporaneous records rather than rely on anecdotal conversations or oral protestations about what you would have done.

For a variety of reasons, it is prudent for team leaders to formalise record-keeping. The following are suggestions for areas of focus:

- Records of instructions – who was the client, start and (where relevant) end date, scope of the retainer.
- Records of exceptions – audit trail to show where agreement has been reached to act in a way that is inconsistent with the team's policies, controls and procedures.

4 SRA Code of Conduct for Firms, paragraph 2.2, www.sra.org.uk/solicitors/standards-regulations/code-conduct-firms/.
5 SRA Code of Conduct for Solicitors, RELs and RFLs, paragraph 7.2, www.sra.org.uk/solicitors/standards-regulations/code-conduct-solicitors/.

- Records of breaches of (1) business and employment-related duties (2) STaRs (3) the team's own policies.
- Supervision records.
- Training records.
- Records to show the updating of the team's own policies.

Added to this is the recommendation that team leaders and supervisors (both of whom might be held personally accountable by the SRA for the actions of others) should impress upon colleagues the need to properly record instructions, actions and decisions, so that evidence is contained in the case management systems to support and justify actions. The sense of insisting that there is evidence in the form of attendance notes, confirmatory emails and similar should not be overlooked.

Training programmes

In recent history the SRA has abandoned the traditional methods of ensuring life-long learning through an hours-based response. This annual 16 hours of continuing professional development regime was abandoned in 2016. Instead, solicitors are now required to demonstrate their continuing competency, specifically at the point of applying for their annual practising certificate, but at any time at the behest of the regulator.

This means that solicitors must regularly review their own practising skills, identify and action any learning and development needs, and then make an annual declaration to the SRA about what they have done. The SRA provides assistance through the publication of the Statement of Solicitor Competence. Of course, having appropriate and up to date legal knowledge is a competency that must be maintained. Additional areas of competence are labelled as ethics, professionalism and judgement, working with other people and managing themselves and their own work.

In other words, the regulatory expectation is that a solicitor has more than simply good technical knowledge. For in-house counsel, competency might be demonstrated by acquiring "an adequate understanding of the commercial, organisational and financial context in which they work and their role in it".[6] This can be developed through induction training, reading business policies, shadowing work colleagues from other parts of the business and similar techniques.

Competency might also be met by "understanding and applying the ethical concepts which govern their role and behaviour as a lawyer"[7] and drafting team policies, leading team training on ethics or adopting a role as the team's compliance champion and ensuring that there is an adequate understanding of regulatory and ethical duties. In other words, the range of methods that now can be used to demonstrate continuing competency are wide and no longer necessarily obtained purely through traditional learning techniques or a specific hours-based acquisition of knowledge and skills.

Demonstrating continuing competency is the responsibility of individual solicitors but given that most teams will have a coordinated response to learning and development, and the bulk renewal of practising certificates, it makes sense that there is a standardised way of collecting personal information about competency exercises. In-house team leaders will want to ensure that the following objectives are achieved:

- The employer understands this regulatory requirement and supports it through the provision of appropriate and adequate resources (both in respect of budget and time).
- Individual solicitors understand their personal accountability to demonstrate continuing competence.
- The position with regard to the maintenance of learning and development records; individual solicitors should have documented records on development objectives, the process by which these will be achieved and reflection about whether this has happened.

---

6 Statement of Solicitor Competence, para D3a, www.sra.org.uk/solicitors/resources/cpd/competence-statement/.
7 Statement of Solicitor Competence, para A1b, www.sra.org.uk/solicitors/resources/cpd/competence-statement/.

- A procedure to tie the individual duty into a team-wide and consistent approach.

The SRA has produced resources, including record-keeping templates, in a CPD toolkit available from the SRA website.[8]

The savvy in-house counsel will use this regulatory requirement to their personal advantage rather than simply seeing it as a means to an end and the way of continuing to secure a practising certificate. Using competency requirements to add to skillsets is a way of ensuring that worth as an employee is consolidated. Collectively, a well-trained team of lawyers will add greater value to the business which employs them.

In many ways, in-house counsel have advantages to develop competencies in an innovative way that might not be possible in private practice, and the continuing competency model enables this to happen. Internally, they have access to the wider business, there is usually a learning and development function to assist, and of course there are external lawyers who are often willing to deliver training and updates.

THOUGHT LEADERSHIP

*In this thought leader piece, we hear from **Dan Kayne**. Dan is employed by Network Rail as general counsel (regions). He has been instrumental in developing a learning concept which will resonate with in-house counsel. It is called 'the O Shaped Lawyer' and is described below, together with Dan's observations about the education of lawyers.*

The O Shaped Lawyer

The O Shaped Lawyer was formed in early 2019. When trying to hire lawyers into the legal team at Network Rail, Dan Kayne (General

---

8 SRA Useful information, www.sra.org.uk/solicitors/resources/cpd/tool-kit/useful-information/.

Counsel Regions) noticed a worrying trend. The overwhelming majority of candidates who were interviewed demonstrated exceptional technical lawyering skills but were lacking in the more human-centric skills that were so vital for the role. Dan agreed with his group general counsel that what the team needed were all-rounders, hence the 'O' Shape.

Dan had been frustrated with the myopic focus of the legal profession on technical and intellectual excellence for some time. The fundamental role that human-centric skills play in successful modern-day leaders has largely been ignored. Much of this has to do with the way lawyers are educated through universities and law schools, where black letter law remains the predominant focus.

The struggle to hire suitable lawyers into the team brought Dan's frustrations to a head. He believes that the legal profession is struggling to find its way. Big law remains incredibly profitable but with that comes significant collateral – a lack of diversity, poor mental health, antiquated practices, a lack of trust and disgruntled clients. Many organisations are looking to disrupt the profession, but they have largely centred on technology and process – all very much needed – but, in his opinion, nowhere has there been a movement to make the profession more 'human'.

The 5 Os and the 12 attributes

The 5 Os framework was created as a memorable way to showcase the critical role of human-centric skills. **O**pen minded, **O**riginal, **O**pportunist, **O**wnership and **O**ptimism have since become the guiding principles which define the O Shaped Lawyer programme. Below, Dan explains more.

Figure 1: The 5 Os framework

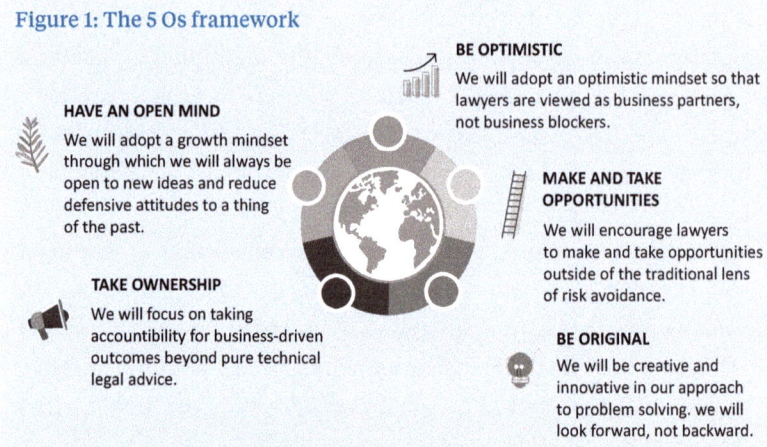

BE OPTIMISTIC
We will adopt an optimistic mindset so that lawyers are viewed as business partners, not business blockers.

HAVE AN OPEN MIND
We will adopt a growth mindset through which we will always be open to new ideas and reduce defensive attitudes to a thing of the past.

MAKE AND TAKE OPPORTUNITIES
We will encourage lawyers to make and take opportunities outside of the traditional lens of risk avoidance.

TAKE OWNERSHIP
We will focus on taking accountibility for business-driven outcomes beyond pure technical legal advice.

BE ORIGINAL
We will be creative and innovative in our approach to problem solving. we will look forward, not backward.

I started to share my thinking with my peer group and then more widely at industry roundtables and conferences, each time building more support and momentum for the creation of a more human-centric profession. This led to a series of interviews with leading general counsel from FTSE 250 companies and the subsequent publication of a report[9] that gave resounding endorsement to the contention that lawyers' skillsets are largely inadequate and out of touch with the modern-day requirements of general counsel, the buyers of their services.

The report distilled the interviews down into three buckets (Building Relationships, Creating Value and Being Adaptable) containing 12 attributes that reflected the skills required of the modern-day lawyer. Technical lawyering is regarded as a given and it was the development of these O Shaped Attributes that would define the next generation of lawyers. The report made the profession sit up and take notice and was the precursor to much of the progress that the O Shaped Lawyer programme has made since.

9 (https://static1.squarespace.com/static/5e73266f0be3ab3148757f25/t/5e736114824
c026bd67da1e1/1584619820423/O+Shaped+Lawyer+-+In-House+Report+%28Febru
ary+2020%29.pdf.)

Figure 2: The 12 attributes

	EMPATHY	INFLUENCE	COMMUNICATION	COLLABORATE
BUILD RELATIONSHIPS	The skill to understand perspectives and agendas of other people	The skill to change the actions or mindsets of others	The skill to deliver the right message to a given audience	The skill to work effectively with people both in the short and long term
	IDENTIFY	SOLVE	SYNTHESISE	SIMPLIFY
CREATE VALUE	The skill to see business opportunities in the face of legal challenges	The skill to find the optimal legal solution to a given business opportunity or challenge	The skill to form sound judgements combining information and determining importance	The skill to distil the most critical elements into an easy to understand form
	COURAGE	RESILIENCE	FEEDBACK	CONTINOUS LEARNING
BE ADAPTABLE	The skill to take action in the face of fear or uncertainty	The skill to recover quickly from disappointment or setback	The skill to seek out information to identify areas for improvement	The skill to apply new skills, techniques and information in practice

The legal ecosystem

Despite the emergence of the disruptors over the last decade, the fundamentals remain the same – it is a profession that is inherently inefficient, lacks genuine customer centricity, is steeped in tradition and attracts, promotes and rewards the same type of behaviours and practices it has always done. Whereas the disruptors have generally focused on a particular part of the profession (such as in-house or private practice), the O Shaped Lawyer programme has adopted a whole system approach to transform the profession.

Take legal education – outdated and focused on academic excellence rather than preparing aspiring lawyers for the world of legal practice. It's currently undergoing a once in a generation change in the UK, due to commence in autumn 2021, but despite eight years in the making, with consultation across the industry, the main working groups failed to include in-house lawyers – the people that buy the services that the law schools are supposed to be preparing for practice.

Law schools have suffered from the same narrow focus. Before our programme's involvement, law schools had been designing their courses for the new SQE alongside their law firm clients, but with no involvement with the in-house legal community. It has culminated in a course (the Solicitors Qualifying Exam or SQE) that places even less emphasis on the skills elements which were already falling short.

When you look at the different parts of the profession in isolation, you recognise that whilst the O Shaped Lawyer programme ambition to transform legal education might seem like a worthwhile and noble cause, it would only be setting up the next generation of lawyers for an even bigger fall if we left our ambitions there. By taking a holistic view, we saw that embedding human-centric skills in law school curricula would only increase the appetite for aspiring lawyers to develop and focus on these critical skills when they started life in practice. As it stands, they would likely be disappointed as the profession wouldn't be able to satisfy that appetite. It means that the O Shaped Lawyer programme must be the trigger for change across the whole profession, not just education, so that the next generation of lawyers can build on and enhance the skills training that we are pushing so hard for at law schools.

People first, then lawyers

From the outset of the O, the mantra of "people first, then lawyers" has been core to our philosophy. Few would associate the legal profession with compassion, kindness and caring, it being better known for long hours, command and control styles of leadership and a phenomenal record of financial success driven largely by a culture of fear of failure. To many in the profession, the idea of displaying emotion, particularly something like compassion, would be uncomfortable and seen as a weakness that few would want to expose.

The legal profession needs to start looking after its people. Too often we have heard about law firm profit margins growing because these assets are being made to sweat. It's a significant contributory factor for a mental health record that ranks lowest of all the professions and an external perception of the profession as lacking in warmth, compassion and trust.

There is plenty of evidence which shows that a more compassionate approach from the leadership of an organisation leads to a more loyal, engaged, workforce and that will ultimately financially benefit the organisation too. Whilst the focus remains on Profit Per Equity Partner (PEP) and profits, shifting mindsets to a more purpose-driven profession will be incredibly difficult and will only happen if the growing community of general counsel backing the programme demand it.

The importance of general counsel in driving the change

As the O Shaped Lawyer report of February 2020 reflected the views of some of the most high-profile general counsel in the UK, it allowed the O Shaped Lawyer programme to share its vision around the profession with an increasing degree of credibility. It made the doubters listen and more progressive parts of the profession get behind its messaging and endorse its ambition.

Since its publication, the O Shaped group has built an ever-growing community of general counsel, heads of legal and in-house legal operations specialists to build the case for change around the O Shaped attributes. It is this group which has the capability and the influence to drive and embed the change.

Although many in-house teams are looking to adopt the O Shaped attributes as part of their internal development as well as their relationships with external law firms, the biggest and most powerful impact has been when major corporates have included the requirement for O Shaped attributes to be demonstrated as part of a request for proposal process. This has an immediate and profound impact with the law firms.

The O Shaped Lawyer programme has sought to connect the profession to effect change to the entire legal system. The significance of high-profile and influential general counsel endorsing the programme cannot be underestimated. As buyers of legal services in a £35 billion per annum industry, their voices carry significant weight. Law firms listen and consequently the curriculums at law schools, driven by the needs of law firms, are being modernised to reflect the broader range of skills so vital to our next generation of lawyers.

Sustainable change

The programme team recognised that to have a sustainable impact, it needed to move on from the research and the sharing of its vision to making it a reality. The profession's interest may have been piqued but for there to be a lasting impact, there needed to be real and tangible progress. Like anything else (including the technical skills where lawyers are such high achievers) these skills need to be practised regularly and consistently. You can't become an O Shaped Lawyer overnight. For these skills to become pervasive, they need to form part of everyday activity of lawyers and aspiring lawyers from early education through to the most senior leadership positions in the profession.

Legal practice – the O Shaped pilots

To embed the thinking into practice, the programme team have run a series of six-month pilots between law firms and in-house teams which are designed to focus on how legal services are provided as well as what is being delivered. To achieve this, they set up small, psychologically safe working groups where in-house lawyers and their external partners openly discuss the attributes in the context of real work and consider collectively how they can improve their services to best meet the needs of the business.

Legal training

In 2020, the O Shaped Lawyer programme partnered with one of the biggest law schools in the UK, the University of Law, to design and deliver a number of O Shaped introductory courses for junior lawyers. Participants are taken through the attributes in a practical, focused way, allowing them to take lessons away and start applying them in practice immediately. This was a first of its kind in any law school in the UK and has proved to be exceptionally popular with further introductory courses planned for 2021.

The future

COVID-19 has brought the messaging of our programme into sharper focus. The profession has been forced into a dramatic change, having to, overnight, move away from a culture of presenteeism to one of flexibility and empowerment. As a result, there are more open conversations than ever before and genuine concern for the health and well-being of colleagues and their loved ones. It means that the changes we have been advocating for are being listened to and the likelihood of more widespread adoption is becoming a reality.

Conclusion

Top quality technical legal skills will always be an essential ingredient for high-achieving lawyers. Soon though, expect to see human-centric skills featuring far more prominently across all parts of the profession. From aspiring lawyers at law school all the way through to senior partners in law firms and in-house teams in corporates, the O Shaped Lawyer programme team is committed to delivering against its vision of making the profession better for those who are in it, those who use it and those who are joining it.

Top tips for in-house legal leaders

- ✔ Manage the business's expectations about what the legal team is able to do.
- ✔ Protect the team with a good governance framework and usable policies, controls and procedures.
- ✔ Keep team structure charts and reporting lines up to date.
- ✔ Be visible to the business and to your team.
- ✔ Ensure effective communication of your expectations.
- ✔ Ensure effective communication of your support.
- ✔ Make sure that supervision works and is working in practice.
- ✔ Train and develop your colleagues.

Chapter IX:
Setting the tone (2)
The lone in-house counsel

Be very clear that the SRA expects to see the demonstration of compliance with regulatory and ethical duties in practice. It does not take kindly to template-based compliance, or a tick-box attitude, or lip service to regulatory needs. Instead, it is entitled to see evidence that in-house counsel have responded to their own particular environment and can demonstrate that they have the infrastructure and skill sets which suit this setting and allows them to deliver good quality legal services in a way that is compatible with the need to uphold the standards and principles stipulated in the STaRs.

The response from an in-house counsel who is the only regulated individual in their business will not be the same as the response from the in-house counsel who heads up, or otherwise has a senior or supervisory role, in a legal team. The lone in-house counsel's response is unlikely to warrant the production of copious policies, but rather clarity about the responsibilities of the role and, as importantly, the limits of the role.

There is a risk that being the only regulated person (or at least the only person regulated in respect of the provision of legal services) will lead to misunderstandings about how this status makes the individual different to other work colleagues. While all colleagues are bound together by employment contracts, business objectives and a business operational model, in-house counsel must also ensure that their regulated status is catered for, and not put in jeopardy, by their surroundings.

Some suggestions as to what lone in-house counsel should prioritise in terms of their conversations with their employer include:

- A written job description which the individual is satisfied is an accurate reflection of what they can do for their employer.
- An understanding of the outer limits of in-house counsel's competency. The employer may naively assume that a solicitor should be able to turn their hand to every sort of legal services, but the risks attached to being a 'jack of all trades' are obvious, both in terms of breaching SRA competency expectations plus negligence issues. It is incumbent on the lawyer to educate the employer as to their own skill sets and areas of expertise.
- A policy on outsourcing legal services: control of the process, budgetary agreement, acknowledgement of in-house counsel's ongoing role etc.
- A statement to explain regulatory and ethical duties which must be met by the individual: when counsel cannot act, the position with regard to conflicts of interest and conflicts of duties etc.
- Clarity about undertakings and what in-house counsel will and will not do.
- Discussion about the indemnity position of the lone counsel.

"While all colleagues are bound together by employment contracts, business objectives and a business operational model, in-house counsel must also ensure that their regulated status is catered for, and not put in jeopardy, by their surroundings."

Undertakings – some extra thoughts

We first discussed undertakings in Chapter V. It is worth revisiting this topic and exploring it from the perspective of the lone professional in a commercial business or, to be more blunt and bold, the only individual who is bound by SRA oversight in this area.

The giving and receiving of an undertaking is riddled with regulatory potholes. In particular, it is important that in-house counsel understands how their regulatory position changes adversely immediately they give an undertaking, or even if someone else thinks that they have received an undertaking and they have relied upon this, even if that was not the intention.

Breaching an undertaking is a serious regulatory issue; as a professional person you have broken your word, and this will undermine and compromise fundamental principles such as trust and confidence in the profession and personal integrity. Because of the risks associated with the dishonouring of an undertaking, it is important to be clear that a solicitor is never under any compulsion to provide one.

The regulatory definition of an undertaking is as follows: "a statement, given orally or in writing, whether or not it includes the word 'undertake' or 'undertaking', to someone who reasonably places reliance on it, that you or a third party will do something or cause something to be done, or refrain from doing something".[1]

The conduct duty is described in paragraph 1.3 of the SRA Code of Conduct and is as follows: "you perform all undertakings given by you, and do so within an agreed timescale or if no timescale has been agreed then within a reasonable amount of time".[2]

This is unforgiving language. Bear in mind the following points:

- An undertaking is a binding promise.
- An oral statement may be construed as an undertaking.
- You might give an undertaking without saying or writing the words 'undertake' or 'undertaking'.

---

1 SRA Glossary, www.sra.org.uk/solicitors/standards-regulations/glossary/.
2 www.sra.org.uk/solicitors/standards-regulations/code-conduct-solicitors/.

- Generally, ambiguity favours the recipient who placed reliance on it.
- An in-house counsel's undertaking is personally binding on them and not their employer.

In other words, reliance on an in-house counsel's undertaking might be convenient for the employer and precarious for the solicitor concerned. The solicitor is best advised to pre-empt any misunderstandings by having appropriate confirmatory conversations with their employer about what they are prepared to do.

If prepared to give an undertaking, then risk management techniques should be documented, such as:

- Clarity about the circumstances in which an undertaking will be given.
- Having confidence that the undertaking is realistic and can be performed by the giver.
- Evidence to show that the undertaking is supported by the instructing client.
- Ensuring that there is an agreed formula for the giving of undertakings so that they are in writing and with clear language to identify the extent of the undertaking and the timescales involved.
- Appropriate record-keeping including the noting of the undertaking and diarising to ensure it is not forgotten.

Indemnity considerations

In-house counsel are not required to comply with the SRA Indemnity Insurance Rules and have compulsory professional indemnity insurance. In this way they are different from private practitioners, as authorised entities must comply with the SRA Indemnity Insurance Rules and have mandatory levels of professional indemnity insurance as a condition of continuing authorisation.

The SRA advises the employers of in-house counsel that this is the case and that they may wish to consider insurance as they are vicariously liable for the actions of their employees.[3] This is nothing more than a helpful nudge as the SRA cannot force unauthorised employers to indemnify in-house counsel.

As this cannot be remedied, in-house counsel are left in a potentially hazardous and insecure position. Consequently, it is another of the discussions which should not be avoided, and which should be had regularly during the employment relationship: what happens to me, if I make a mistake? What happens if I am subject to a regulatory investigation and need to finance my defence? Will I be protected? Clearly the answer is no, unless the employer provides an adequate indemnity, or the individual acquires their own source of protection.

THOUGHT LEADERSHIP

*The following thought leader piece is contributed by **Fergal Cathie**, partner, and **Michael Clark**, legal director, of Clyde & Co LLP's professional disputes and regulatory group, and reflects further on this dilemma.*

Solicitors in private practice, providing legal services to the public – usually in law firms – are required to carry a minimum level of professional indemnity insurance to cover the risk of claims being brought by clients or third parties to recover losses, usually arising out of negligent advice or similar breaches of duty.

Many law firms also carry insurance to cover the costs of dealing with regulatory investigations and some types of disciplinary process, but it is important to note that this is not part of the compulsory insurance regime, and the practice is not universal. Importantly, there is no requirement that in-house solicitors should carry insurance (their

---

3   SRA Guidance, 'Unregulated organisations for employers of SRA regulated lawyers', www. sra.org.uk/solicitors/guidance/unregulated-organisations-employers-sra-regulated-lawyers/.

internal 'clients' being their employers). And even solicitors in private practice may not always be covered for regulatory investigations or disciplinary processes where these touch on issues which arise outside the workplace.

This does give rise to potential issues, particularly for those who work in-house, and it is therefore important to be aware of how exposures might arise.

An in-depth regulatory investigation may require protracted engagement with the SRA, sometimes over several years. Hundreds of thousands of documents may be involved and, if a matter proceeds to prosecution in the SDT, there may be a trial, lasting days or even weeks. The costs of instructing experienced professional advisers to respond to investigations and defend proceedings can be very considerable, and it is not uncommon for defence costs to run into hundreds of thousands of pounds – or more – when careers are on the line.

Some employers will carry Directors' and Officers' liability insurance (or other management liability insurance), but it is by no means clear that this would cover all individual members of the general counsel's office, if they are not sufficiently senior within the organisation or do not have management responsibilities. Further, whereas an employer will usually be vicariously liable for the negligent acts of an employee, in the regulatory sphere it is the individual who carries personal responsibility for acts of misconduct. It may be that some employers will be content to assist with funding the defence of an employed solicitor. But ideally this ought to be addressed in the contract of employment, and in-house solicitors should consider asking for an indemnity as part of their employment terms in relation to regulatory exposures, as well as employment liabilities, when joining an organisation.

The matter can become more complicated when one moves to a new employer. Regulatory investigations can often have a 'long tail': enquiries can sometimes be instigated years after the conduct under scrutiny takes place. If you are prosecuted for conduct which took place while you were at company A, but you now work for company B, who will fund your defence? What if company A is no longer trading? What if you have retired?

All of this points to the need to reflect carefully on one's personal responsibilities as a solicitor. If there is any doubt over the availability of an indemnity, or as to whether insurance covers you as an individual in your own right, you might be well advised to seek specialist input from an insurance broker with experience in professional liability and regulation.

Top tips for lone in-house counsel

- ✔ Ensure that you have an accurate contract and job description.
- ✔ Be prepared to tackle inappropriate expectations about what you can and will do.
- ✔ More than this, be explicit about what you can't and won't do for your employer and the business.
- ✔ Understand the fallout if regulatory expectations and ethical behaviours are not achieved – the SRA looks to you because it cannot look at the employer.
- ✔ Identify and be comfortable with the various scenarios where your employer's expectations place your regulated status at risk.
- ✔ Protect yourself and your regulated status.

THOUGHT LEADERSHIP

Chris Stait, the legal director of Digital Catapult, answered the following questions to show how his in-house role has developed.

Q: Can you provide a brief description of your career history, ie, when you were admitted, your specialisms and types of employment prior to joining Digital Catapult?

A. I was admitted in 2011. I'm a general commercial counsel but have specialised in the legal areas of state aid, public procurement and intellectual property law; but I would say I'm actually a solution-driven technology lawyer, who has refined the ability to sit across all functions of the business and pragmatically and efficiently solve problems and influence decision making with a broad legal and business toolkit. Prior to Digital Catapult, I worked at GKN (FTSE 100 automotive and engineering company) as its Group IP counsel, and prior to GKN, I trained and qualified in private practice where I worked in my firm's science and technology department.

Q: When did you join Digital Catapult?

A. I joined Digital Catapult in 2018.

Q: What services does your employer deliver?

A. Digital Catapult is one of a network of non-profit private sector research technology organisations that were established by the UK government. Its mission is to advance the adoption of advanced digital technology in the UK, eg, Future Networks (including 5G and IOT), AI and Immersive Technology. Digital Catapult offers advanced digital solutions and opportunities to achieve this mission, including technology development, innovation services, ecosystem mapping and engagement, acceleration programmes, infrastructure access and deployment and collaborative research and development. We tend to look at this as partnering, rather than services/sales, as our goal is creating the biggest possible impact for our partners and stakeholders rather than being profit driven.

Q: **What types of legal services do you deliver and to whom (ie, who are your clients)?**

A. *Legal services*: company secretarial; compliance (excluding health and safety); data protection management; company policies and procedures; contracting.

Clients (everyone): board; executive/senior management; heads of department and heads of technology; most other staff working on projects/programmes; other internal service providers (IT/HR/finance etc). In short, the legal (and procurement) team is highly accessible.

Q: **Who – if anyone – legally qualified or not, or support staff, is in your team?**

A. I have two members in my procurement team (non-lawyers) and a paralegal (law degree) in my legal team. I'm currently recruiting a junior solicitor.

Q: **How do you see your role as legal director?**

A. I see my role as: maximising value in interactions and contracting; managing risk in contracting and legal matters, advising senior management and providing options; compliance; having a moral compass – doing the right thing, being seen to do the right thing, holding everyone to the same standard, being approachable to allow others to report issues and have them resolved; problem solving and being a solution provider – if someone doesn't know whether or what to do outside their own department, they often end up coming to legal; strategic operations – where there's an irregular or non-standard project, I'll structure and coordinate the solution.

Q: **How do your colleagues see your role as legal director?**

A. I believe most of my colleagues would view my role simply as contracting and compliance. Perhaps a very small minority see it as simply a barrier or hurdle to overcome, but these tend to be colleagues that have a focused KPI-driven view of their own roles or lack the experience to appreciate that the quickest pathway to full resolution isn't necessarily the quickest to complete the immediate task. Some, but I don't believe enough, see or understand the work done to achieve better outcomes and strategically structure arrangements (but I need to free up time to communicate this effectively).

Q: What conversations have you had with other members of the organisation about your regulated status?

A. I generally try to keep things simple. Unless it's specifically required, I don't differentiate between legal, regulatory, company or policy and my own department's requirements on a matter. On occasion, I have had to say "no" for regulatory reasons, eg, a request to provide legal services to help a third party. Helpfully I work under the CFO who has regulatory duties, and so the profession over any one job is firmly understood, and I'm well supported in holding the line.

Q: Do you have documented policies, controls and procedures?

A. Yes, we're moving to an organisation size which requires more of this type of documentation and has been updated and supplemented since I arrived. I believe this to be vital to help give structure and certainty to the business. The business user should always be first in mind when drafting and implementing these.

Q: What is your view of the role of in-house counsel in terms of creating the right environment for ethical behaviour within the business?

A. I think they go hand in hand and it's an important role of the legal department. Legal are often best placed to understand general business ethics and compliance, to see issues with our breadth of involvement across departments or silos, identify gaps and resolve problems. Our professional requirements demand ethical behaviour, with a duty above that of any particular job or role, unlike most other employees. That naturally provides a firm base for a strong legal department to provide the moral compass for the organisation. There's a virtuous circle, with colleagues feeling they can trust you, not only with their problems, but that issues will be handled fairly, with discretion, and not just swept under the carpet, no matter how difficult.

- -

Q: What are the challenges of being an in-house legal adviser?

A. My biggest challenge is getting early input into strategic direction of projects and programmes. This can add significant value but requires (1) that aspect of the role to be sold to the business, and (2) making the time to have that input (including building the relationships and understanding, to get you access by default). Making time for the strategic work when there is so much delivery required is also a challenge, along with building the trust and confidence of stakeholders that you're not a barrier or a drag on progress, but an important part of getting the business working well.

- -

Q: What advice would you give to someone who has recently been appointed in a similar position to your role?

A. Take the time to know and understand the business – the drivers and the cost centres; find your key stakeholders and understand their perceptions, needs, desires and priorities; build and manage your compliance allies and build and support the credibility of the function at senior, executive and board levels – a direct relationship with the Audit Committee is helpful; be approachable and ensure you're known across the business – you'll get insight and intelligence that you otherwise wouldn't achieve.

- -

Q: Do your colleagues understand the implications of working with a regulated lawyer?

A. I would say mostly no, not directly; it's the application of it of which they are aware (but they probably don't know or don't differentiate between policies, procedures, laws and regulatory issues). Senior management are aware that I've assumed the moral compass as well as managing, and helping to manage, risk. The CFO is aware and fully supportive, and acts as a good sounding board as well as a point of escalation if needed.

Chapter X:
In-house counsel in the boardroom

Access to the board and advice to the board

In a bygone era, before the SRA came into existence, the Law Society of England and Wales was the regulator of solicitors and latterly published its *Guide to the Professional Conduct of Solicitors* to deliver its regulatory and ethical expectations. This contained the following direction: "A solicitor employed as the senior legal adviser of a company or a local authority must have direct access to the board or to the council and its committees."[1]

---

1 The Law Society, *The Guide to the Professional Conduct of Solicitors*, 8th edition, Law Society Publishing, 1999, rule 4.08.

Commentary was added to the statement to suggest that a solicitor employed in this position should seek to ensure that their employment terms provided for this access, and that the reference to "direct access" was in the context of where such access might be necessary.

Such forceful and instructional wording is not in keeping with the SRA's style of regulation and there is nothing so direct as this to support in-house counsel in respect of their relationships with others, except by implication in the Principles and the SRA Code. However, access to the board – and/or the owners of the business – should be afforded to the business's lawyers. Direct access for senior in-house counsel is the best practice position which should be achieved.

In-house counsel should have access to the board and the senior management team, either directly on the part of the senior lawyers, or indirectly via the senior lawyers for everyone else fulfilling a legal function. This is essential. If lawyers have the role of the ethical heartbeat or conscience of the business, then access to the head of the business is vital. The head needs to know what is happening and be given impartial, best interests information.

This might challenge counsel; it necessitates the need to address and confront inappropriate behaviours rather than turn a blind eye. This is perhaps made easier to consider if it is always kept in mind that in-house counsel's client is the business, rather than the individuals within it, and in-house counsel have an obligation to their client to protect their interests.

Recognising this function is another illustration of the duty incumbent on in-house counsel to act in a way that supports principled behaviour as described in the STaRs.

Integrity, as we know, is a behaviour expected of all solicitors and is seen as a characteristic of the profession. It is an invaluable trait in a commercial environment. Without expressing this specifically, it is one of the attributes which business owners are likely to want, need and expect from their in-house lawyers.

There are many ways to describe what it means to act with integrity but for these purposes, the words of W. Clement Stone, an American

"In-house counsel should have access to the board and the senior management team, either directly on the part of the senior lawyers, or indirectly via the senior lawyers for everyone else fulfilling a legal function. This is essential."

businessman and philanthropist, are apposite. He explained integrity by saying: "Have the courage to say no. Have the courage to face the truth. Do the right thing because it is right."[2]

Demonstrating integrity in this environment requires in-house counsel to also display independence. No one should be able to fetter or influence or alter counsel's ability to give impartial advice to the client in any particular instructions. It also requires a consideration of own interest conflicts, actual conflicts and circumstances where there is a significant risk of a conflict arising. If there is anything, or anyone, which compromises impartiality, then conduct duties trigger the need for the conflicted lawyer not to act. Own interest questions might arise because of the individual's own employment, or in matters concerning relationships with other employees, as well as through outside interests.

In-house counsel as company secretary

Of course, a company secretary does not have to be legally trained, but it is an obvious addition to in-house counsel's role for them to act as company secretary. Having this job title does not mean that the counsel title can be forgotten. In-house counsel who also act as company secretary must have their legal hat firmly on their heads at all times and bring the same principled behaviour to this role as they would to their legal services output.

Where the role of company secretary is fulfilled by a non-lawyer, it is important the senior counsel have the ability to understand and intervene in any behaviours which are likely to compromise their client. This is one of the circumstances in which having direct access to the board, as described in the previous section, is sensible. It is also sensible to have discussions and cement the actual role of in-house counsel *vis-à-vis* the secretary to avoid any misunderstandings or gaps in service.

2   www.quotes.net/quote/50896.

A seat on the board

The appeal, or the goal, of in-house commercial practice is often a seat at the board, which brings the giddy collision of law and commerce to the occupant. The alternative view is that this a position which has the potential to cause strife between regulatory and ethical duties and duties with a purer employment focus or even a self-interest perspective.

The SRA does not (and probably could not, even if it wanted to) prohibit a solicitor from taking a seat at the board. Bearing in mind that board members are commercial decision makers, it is prudent that a solicitor on the board explains the tensions that will arise if board actions create a conflict with their own individual regulatory and ethical duties.

In practical terms, there ought to be an agreement about how the board role will work with the legal advisory role, resources available to support the incumbent, and their indemnity position in the event that anything about this role creates personal difficulties.

Taking an ownership interest

In-house counsel, alongside other employees, might be invited to invest in their employer's business or be gifted such an interest. As with seats at the board, there is no regulatory prohibition in having such an ownership interest. However, in-house counsel must again consider and maintain principled behaviour, notwithstanding their interest in the business.

It is more probable that this would trigger the need to consider the position on own interest conflicts as described in paragraph 6.1 of the SRA Code of Conduct for Solicitors,[3] and, for example, ensure that ownership considerations do not create an own interest conflict. There is an absolute prohibition on a solicitor acting in circumstances where

---

3   www.sra.org.uk/solicitors/standards-regulations/code-conduct-solicitors/.

there is an actual, or significant risk, of an own interest conflict arising. It would be prudent to ensure that the business understands in-house counsel's need to make judgement calls in such circumstances, and to understand that this might mean that legal services which could ordinarily be provided in-house have to be outsourced to external legal providers instead.

Chapter XI:

Tensions – working in an international business

Much of the attraction of in-house legal appointments is to be part of a global network; such opportunities are not afforded to many private practitioners outside of the Magic Circle and certain other international law firms.

For the SRA's purposes, the description 'overseas' applies to anywhere that is not practice from an English or Welsh location (on the basis that the SRA is the approved regulator of solicitors of England and Wales).

The regulatory and ethical considerations are considered in this chapter.

Occasional or temporary practice outside England and Wales

Individuals involved in 'fly in, fly out' lawyering assignments, and in-house counsel providing services overseas on a temporary basis, must continue to comply with the SRA's regulatory requirements as if they were providing services domestically. They must comply with the SRA Principles and the SRA Code of Conduct for Solicitors, RELs and RFLs.

Practising overseas as in-house counsel

A solicitor practising overseas on anything other than a temporary basis might need to adhere to a different set of requirements in respect of their behaviours and conduct than those which are relevant to in-house lawyers practising within the jurisdiction.

These requirements are contained in the SRA Overseas and Cross-border Practice Rules[1] which replace the SRA Principles and the SRA Code of Conduct for Solicitors, RELs and RFLs in these circumstances, unless the individual's practice "predominantly comprises the provision of legal services to clients within England and Wales, or in relation to assets located in England and Wales".[2]

This is an important distinction to make. An in-house counsel employed in an overseas location should consider carefully whether they can rely on the disapplication clause. Further assistance with this decision is unlikely to be given by the SRA but they might ask an individual to justify their decision, so it would be prudent to have documented evidence of analysis.

Practising overseas is a defined phrase and for in-house counsel simply means the conduct of a practice "of a solicitor established outside England and Wales for the purpose of providing legal services in an overseas jurisdiction".[3]

---

1 SRA Overseas and Cross-border Practice Rules, www.sra.org.uk/solicitors/standards-regulations/overseas-cross-border-practice-rules/.
2 SRA Overseas and Cross-border Practice Rules, Rule 1.3.
3 SRA Glossary, www.sra.org.uk/solicitors/standards-regulations/glossary/.

Where the Overseas Rules apply, in-house counsel must comply with a tailored version of the SRA Principles[4] which reapply the basic ethical behaviours to an international setting, so that:

You act

1. *in a way that upholds the constitutional principle of the rule of law and the proper administration of justice in England and Wales.*
2. *in a way that upholds public trust and confidence in the **solicitors' ** profession of England and Wales and in legal services provided by authorised **persons**.*
3. *with independence.*
4. *with honesty.*
5. *with integrity.*
6. *in a way that encourages equality, diversity and inclusion having regard to the legal, regulatory and cultural context in which you are **practising overseas.***
7. *in the best interests of each client.*

Overseas Principle 6 is significant as it acknowledges that there might be different legal, regulatory and cultural norms in the jurisdiction and that these must be considered. It would be advisable to undertake a benchmarking exercise to consider whether there are differences between the domestic and overseas position and counsel's response.

Notwithstanding location, as a regulated individual, in-house counsel's reporting and notification duties still apply, and the Overseas Rules describe the SRA's expectations at Rule 4.

Dependent on the size of the overseas team, consideration should be given to the development of policies, controls and procedures as well as appropriate terms in individual employment contracts. Working overseas only adds to the SRA interest in what the individual does;

---

4 www.sra.org.uk/solicitors/standards-regulations/overseas-cross-border-practice-rules/.

"*Working overseas only adds to the SRA interest in what the individual does; bearing in mind its concerns about reputational risks and that overseas practitioners could be described as ambassadors for the SRA and the solicitor brand.*"

bearing in mind its concerns about reputational risks and that overseas practitioners could be described as ambassadors for the SRA and the solicitor brand.

Domestic in-house counsel with responsibilities for a global network

In-house counsel based in England and Wales may find that they have governance responsibilities, arising in connection with people and risks, stretching outside of the jurisdiction. They might have legal teams based overseas or they might have responsibility to manage legal and business risks on a global scale.

In these circumstances, it is necessary to ensure that what the SRA has sometimes described as 'global contagion' (ie, anything of a negative nature which might have reputational repercussions for the SRA and their role as an approved regulator and in terms of the reputation of the solicitors' profession) does not have an impact on their regulated reputation. Points to consider:

- Solicitors who supervise others providing legal services have a duty to ensure that there is effective supervision, and they are personally accountable for the actions of these colleagues. Where they manage others, they have duties to consider competency attainment in order to fulfil their personal duties in the SRA Code of Conduct for Solicitors, RELs and RFLs.[5] Are reporting lines properly constructed so that the supervising solicitor is able to fulfil their role effectively, notwithstanding geographical realities?
- Does training of overseas colleagues happen?
- Have policies, controls and procedures designed to deal with client care, service standards and ethical objectives been tailored to suit the needs of the lawyers practising overseas? Are there records of variations to accommodate jurisdictional differences, and is there adequate monitoring for compliance?

5   SRA Code of Conduct for Solicitors, paragraphs 3.5 and 3.6, www.sra.org.uk/solicitors/standards-regulations/code-conduct-solicitors/.

- Where global risk management is the responsibility of in-house counsel, do they have access to the information which is necessary for performance? Are there effective reporting lines and internal communication strategies?

A note about cross-border practice – watch this space

In this chapter we have referenced the SRA Overseas and Cross-border Practice Rules. A word of caution is needed about cross-border practice. The Cross-border Practice Rules apply in the context of European Union professional activities. They apply if lawyers in one member state engage in professional activities in another member state which is a member of the Council of Bars and Law Societies of Europe. The Rules were drafted at a time when the United Kingdom was a European Union member state and have not (at the time of writing this book) been updated to reflect that the UK is now a third state.

Chapter XII:
The scope for other activities

The growth of in-house counsel's client base

A significant change to practising rights was enabled through the introduction of the STaRs in November 2019. Prior to this launch date, in-house counsel had been prohibited by regulatory rules from offering legal services to as wide a client base as private practitioners. In-house counsel were bound by a set of Rules[1] which stated that their default client was their employer, and services to other clients could only be provided if there was some nexus between the employer and these third parties.

---

1 SRA Practice Framework Rules 2011, www.sra.org.uk/solicitors/handbook/.

This did allow in-house counsel to provide legal services to what were described as related bodies and in matters connected with their employment. For example, if employed by a company, the Rules allowed the solicitor to act for other companies within the group structure subject to a consideration that there were no ethical obstacles that prevented them from acting in that client's best interests. This was the limit of the client base, and certainly there was no possibility of providing services to members of the public.

In fact, this regulatory restriction had extended the legal position on the provision of legal services. For this reason, it was removed with the introduction of the STaRs. This means that in-house counsel are now required to comply with legal restrictions only and these restrictions focus on the provision of reserved legal services and the circumstances in which these can be provided to clients.

The law sets a framework and means that in-house counsel can provide reserved legal activities to their employer and related or connected bodies only. This allows in-house counsel to continue to provide such services to non-employer clients where there is a satisfactory nexus between the parties, such as when acting for group companies, joint venture or syndicate transactions or for directors, employees or board members where a matter relates to this employment or office.

As practical tips to ensure compliance, it is prudent to have structure charts to show the relationship between group companies and to keep these updated, and also to understand what services are reserved by statute, and to have clear audit trails when providing services to non-employer clients to justify the decision to act. Conflicts, and significant risks of conflict, must be considered and the duties of confidentiality and disclosure must be fulfilled.

The meaning of reserved legal activities is at section 12 of the Legal Services Act 2007: we are describing the exercise of a right of audience; the conduct of litigation; reserved instrument activities; probate activities; notarial activities and the administration of oaths. It means,

"The law sets a framework and means that in-house counsel can provide reserved legal activities to their employer and related or connected bodies only."

for example, that in-house counsel can provide conveyancing or litigation services (both described in section 12) to their employer and related bodies but not to third parties unconnected with their employer.

Every activity which is not reserved is no longer subject to additional regulatory instructions, meaning in-house counsel can offer certain legal services to members of the public. In this way, in-house counsel's client base has potentially exploded. This means that in some circumstances, in-house counsel can provide services to a wider but still connected client base, or even to members of the public.

This is not as great or as liberating as it may seem. While an employer might welcome the opportunity to exploit this practising right, it is important for in-house counsel to understand that they will be acting as a practising solicitor when delivering legal services. They will be tested against the standards set out in the STaRs, notably the behaviours described in the SRA Principles and the SRA Code of Conduct for Solicitors, RELs and RFLs. This means that the individual will be accountable to their regulatory body and may be asked to prove that they are competent to deliver services to a wider client base. Their employer may see this as a way to further utilise their employees, and to facilitate the provision of legal services to members of the public by their business, and the SRA will have no regulatory reach over them.

Chapter 8 of the SRA Code of Conduct for Solicitors, RELs and RFLs will apply in these circumstances, and in-house counsel will need to:

1. Identify (ie, take steps to ascertain and verify the identity of) the client.
2. Give what is commonly described as client care and terms of business information to the client in an accessible format.
3. Give best possible costs information.
4. Provide written information about how complaints will be handled and written signposting to the Ombudsman service.
5. Resolve complaints within eight weeks or remind the client of their right to seek redress from the Ombudsman.
6. Deal with complaints at no cost to the complainant.

7. Ensure all other information is given to clients in a way that suits them so that they are in a position to make informed decisions.
8. Be responsible for publicity and ensure that it is not misleading.
9. Resist the temptation to solicit business through cold-calling techniques or otherwise make unsolicited approaches to members of the public.
10. Ensure that your clients understand their regulatory protections.

In the event that in-house counsel are requested to provide services to a wider client base, it is sensible to have a toolkit with which to demonstrate compliance, and this will include procedures which are not necessarily part of their employed protocol. These include:

- Client care letter.
- Terms of business or engagement.
- Regulatory information.
- Policies that speak to the risks of providing services to this client base, for example, a conflicts search methodology, privacy and other data protection policies, a website policy, a procedure to ensure that clients are provided with information about any referral arrangements, a complaints handling procedure, and similar.
- Awareness of the SRA Transparency Rules[2] so that if the employer's website refers to the provision of certain legal services, there are references to pricing and service matters.

In addition to the restriction on the provision of reserved legal activities, there are other activities which cannot be provided in this way, for example:

- Financial services can only be provided if the business is authorised by the Financial Conduct Authority.
- Claims management services can only be provided if the business is authorised by the Financial Conduct Authority.

2   www.sra.org.uk/solicitors/standards-regulations/transparency-rules/.

- Immigration work can only be provided if the business is authorised by the Office of the Immigration Services Commissioner.
- Client money cannot be held in a solicitor's client account as this is prohibited by the SRA Code of Conduct for Solicitors, RELs and RFLs.

Providing reserved legal services to members of the public

Subject to certain very specific exemptions, the Legal Services Act 2007 requires a business to be authorised if it provides reserved legal activities to members of the public, or otherwise wishes to provide financial services, claims management or immigration services and is not already regulated for these activities.

The SRA is a licensing body for these purposes and can authorise in-house legal teams to provide reserved legal activities etc to members of the public. This type of entity is described as an alternative business structure or ABS. This term signifies that the ownership and management structure includes non-solicitors, as is now the case with many private practice firms who include non-solicitors in their partnerships and/or external owners.

The ABS is a type of private practice. This format does mean that the SRA has regulatory reach over the employer as well as the lawyer. The owners must be approved, and they will be expected to comply with the SRA Authorisation of Individuals Regulations.[3] In addition, the authorised entity – whether this is the discrete in-house legal team or the larger business – must comply with the Authorisation of Firms Rules[4] and the SRA Code of Conduct for Firms (the Firms Code).[5]

The Firms Code extends conduct and ethical behaviours to all members of the firm. The introduction includes the following statement:

This Code of Conduct describes the standards and business controls that we, the SRA, and the public expect of firms (including sole

---

3 www.sra.org.uk/solicitors/standards-regulations/authorisation-individuals-regulations/.
4 www.sra.org.uk/solicitors/standards-regulations/authorisation-firms-rules/.
5 www.sra.org.uk/solicitors/standards-regulations/code-conduct-firms/.

practices) authorised by us to provide legal services. These aim to create and maintain the right culture and environment for the delivery of competent and ethical legal services to clients.[6]

The introduction also makes clear that the SRA can take disciplinary action against the ABS, and/or its owners and managers, its compliance officers and all employees. Unlike an in-house team, where the SRA has regulatory reach only over the solicitors, the ABS is an entity licensed by the SRA and therefore its regulatory reach is extended. Barristers, legal executives and other alternatively regulated lawyers will find that they can be disciplined by the SRA as well as their own regulators.

The following are examples of disciplinary action taken by the SRA against ABSs:

- The SRA fined Findmyclaims.com Ltd £125,000 for publicity and other STaRs breaches in 2019.[7]
- The SRA fined the Co-operative Legal Services almost £144,000 for recovering improper costs in personal injury matters in 2020.[8]

There are also roles and responsibilities for the managers and owners, and the inclusion of compliance officer roles which must be filled. Chapter 2 describes compliance and business systems so that the ABS must ensure that there is evidence of the following:

- Effective governance structures, arrangements, systems and controls to ensure compliance with SRA arrangements by the firm and all its managers and employees.
- The maintenance of records to demonstrate regulatory compliance.
- The business remains accountable for services performed.
- Financial stability and business viability is actively monitored.
- Risk identification, management and monitoring is undertaken.

6 SRA Code of Conduct for Firms, www.sra.org.uk/solicitors/standards-regulations/code-conduct-firms/.
7 See   www.lawgazette.co.uk/practice/firm-fined-record-124000-for-sending-millions-of-misleading-letters/5069602.article.
8 See   www.lawgazette.co.uk/news/exclusive-co-op-legal-services-to-be-fined-144k-by-sra/5106081.article.

In addition, the firm is required to monitor, and in some cases publish, diversity data and facilitate other arrangements so that legal services are delivered in a safe and appropriate manner.

It is a condition of authorisation that the firm has a Compliance Officer for Legal Practice (a COLP) and a Compliance Officer for Finance and Administration (a COFA) who are approved by the SRA to fulfil these roles. The role description is contained in Chapter 9 of the Firm Code, but the overlap with and accountability of the firm's managers is clearly expressed in Chapter 8.

Many in-house legal teams have taken the decision to seek ABS authorisation. Bearing in mind that this decision means that the entity will be a form of private practice, both the owners and in-house counsel must be satisfied that there is a commercial benefit to this choice as it involves more regulatory interaction with, and oversight of, the whole body.[9]

Pro bono work

Many lawyers choose to offer *pro bono* legal services. For in-house counsel, subject of course to any contractual terms in their employment contracts, offering *pro bono* services might be aligned with the business's corporate and social responsibility strategies.

Nothing about the nature of *pro bono* services should create a situation where there is a slipping of standards or lack of professionalism on the part of the service provider. Regulatory and ethical considerations must be met when delivering *pro bono* legal services as part of the in-house counsel's employment. Bear in mind the following points:

- The variety of legal services offered must be confined to unreserved legal activities in order to avoid breaching the restrictions in the Legal Services Act 2007.

---

9   See Tracey Calvert, *Regulation, Compliance and Ethics in Law Firms*, 2nd Edition, Globe Law and Business, 2020.

- Restrictions also apply that would prevent in-house counsel providing *pro bono* services in connection with claims management, financial services and immigration services.
- When providing legal services, in-house counsel must behave in a manner which is consistent with professional standards and comply with the SRA Principles and other relevant sections of the STaRs.
- Client money cannot be held in connection with *pro bono* services.

If the *pro bono* services are not provided from within the business, but instead by in-house counsel volunteering to work in non-commercial bodies such as law centres or other not-for-profit organisations, the following considerations need to be taken into account:

- These are described as non-commercial bodies (sometimes not-for-profit bodies) under section 23 of the Legal Services Act 2007. Because of a statutory exemption, these types of entity are entitled to offer reserved legal services to the public without the need to be authorised by an approved regulator such as the SRA. This means that solicitors can volunteer to provide *pro bono* services to members of the public and offer *pro bono* services from within a non-commercial body and are not restricted to only providing non-reserved services.
- However, in such circumstances, volunteering solicitors must comply with paragraph 5.6 of the SRA Code of Conduct for Solicitors, RELs and RFLs. In circumstances where the solicitor provides reserved legal services in a non-commercial body, that body must take out and maintain indemnity insurance and this insurance must provide 'adequate and appropriate cover'.
- The SRA Principles and the SRA Code of Conduct for Solicitors will continue to apply to the volunteer solicitor.

- Entities within this sector are entitled to hold client money. In a Statement added to the STaRs,[10] the SRA has confirmed that solicitors working in a non-commercial body are permitted to hold client money in their own name. Unfortunately, the SRA does not define the meaning of 'working' for these purposes and whether this extends to working in a voluntary capacity, so it is prudent to ensure that client monies are held in the name of an employed solicitor rather than a volunteer. Monies held in these circumstances trigger the need to comply with the SRA Accounts Rules 2019.[11]

LawWorks is a charity which promotes *pro bono* legal services and supports solicitors and others when providing such services. With their kind permission, we have been able to reproduce Figure 3 from their practice guidance booklet for solicitors ("Solicitors and *pro bono*: regulatory issues").[12]

External appointments

Solicitors, and others with legal training, are often asked to accept volunteer posts as school governors, on membership committees and similar. It is easy to see why this is the case. With the collective reputation for trustworthiness and integrity that is associated with the legal profession, members of the profession are regarded as valuable contributors.

There are no regulatory restraints on accepting such positions, but it is important that ground rules are established, and personal risks are identified.

For example, while the prospect or expectation of 'on tap' legal advice is part of the attraction for the school or committee in inviting a solicitor to join, boundaries must be set, and caveats explained about

---

10   www.sra.org.uk/solicitors/standards-regulations/hold-client-money/.
11   www.sra.org.uk/solicitors/standards-regulations/accounts-rules/.
12   www.lawworks.org.uk/sites/default/files/files/LawWorks-General-Practice-Regulatory-Guidance-Probono.pdf.

Figure 3: In-house solicitors and *pro bono*: reserved and non-reserved activity

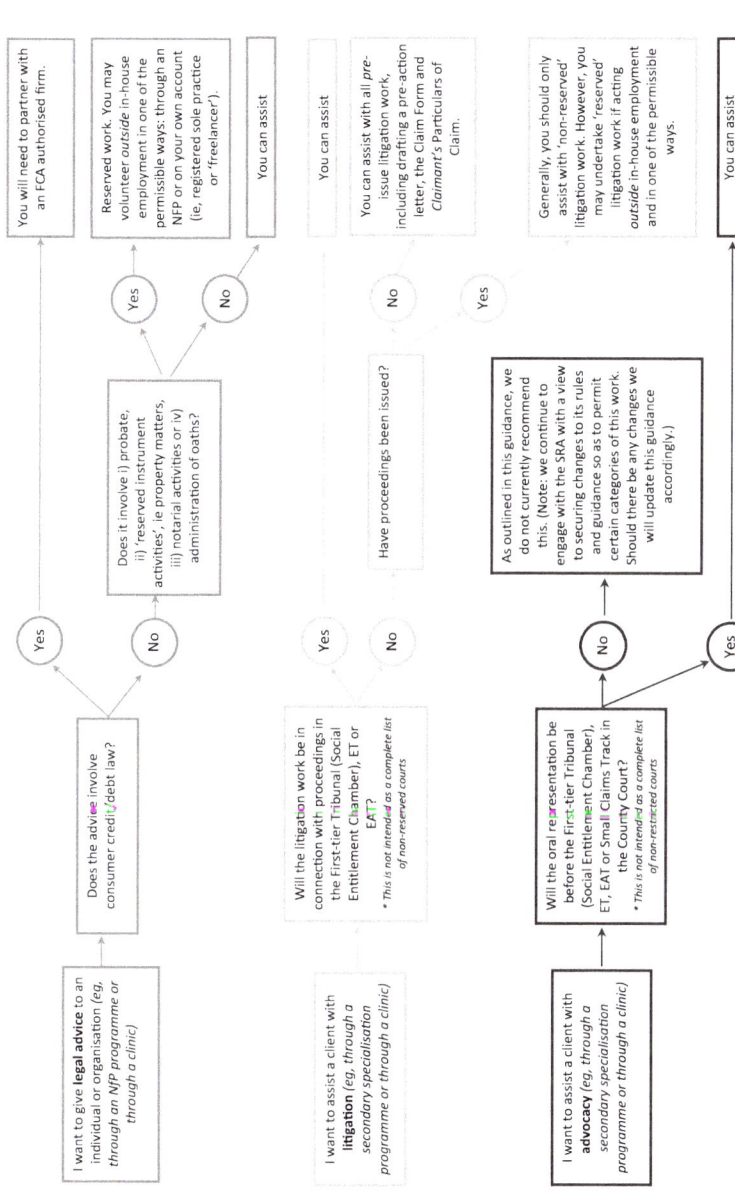

Reproduced with the kind permission of LawWorks, www.lawworks.org.uk.

the extent to which a personally expressed legal opinion can be relied on. Independent legal advice from an indemnified source must always be obtained in circumstances where there is a need to rely on this. No one should assume that the advice which is offered by the legally qualified governor is given in anything other than a personal capacity. Any misunderstandings of this nature are likely to be construed in favour of the recipient of the advice and not the solicitor.

However, and notwithstanding this caveat, the SRA Principles will continue to be relevant to the role holder and their personal conduct. Public interest behaviours are particularly in the spotlight so that any conduct that calls into question duties to uphold the rule of law (Principle 1), duties associated with trust and confidence (Principle 2) and integrity (Principle 5) are likely to be of concern to the SRA which is entitled to pursue regulatory investigations in such circumstances.

The SRA's published Enforcement Strategy[13] confirms the extent of the SRA's interest in an individual's private life and out of office activities. It is worthwhile reading, and the following are key takeaway points:

- The SRA will not deal with any issues relating to the solicitor's competence as a school governor or similar.
- The SRA is concerned with the impact of conduct – and the application of the SRA Principles – if this touches on risk to the delivery of legal services.
- The closer the connection with professional activities, the more seriously the SRA will regard the conduct.
- Examples of topics of concern include financial impropriety, dishonesty and discriminatory behaviour.
- The SRA always investigates criminal convictions, charges or cautions and solicitors have a duty – expressed in paragraph 7.6 of the SRA Code of Conduct for Solicitors, RELs and RFLs – to make prompt reports of such matters.

---

13   SRA Enforcement Strategy, www.sra.org.uk/sra/corporate-strategy/sra-enforcement-strategy/.

- A proportionate approach will be taken to the consideration of criminal matters. The more serious matters are likely to be those relating to dishonesty, fraud, bribery and extortion, terrorism, money laundering, obstructing the course of justice, facilitating or concealing serious or organised criminality by others and matters involving violence, sexual misconduct or child sexual abuse images.

Chapter XIII:

The in-house counsel's role after the COVID-19 pandemic

This book would have had a different ending if it had been written in an age where words like COVID-19, pandemic, social distancing, furloughing and lockdown were not part of our day-to-day vocabulary. However, no one reading this book can have failed to have been affected by the impact of COVID-19, not least in the way that legal services are delivered.

The SRA has been very clear about their expectations of practitioners. To paraphrase their directions: we must do everything we can to maintain high standards and compliance with the SRA Principles and SRA Code; we must have business contingency plans; we must be pragmatic and there is a need to document what we are doing.

In-house counsel are no different to private practitioners in the need to be resilient and adapt to the new order. Unfortunately, your author

"In-house counsel are no different to private practitioners in the need to be resilient and adapt to the new order."

does not have a crystal ball and cannot say when office life will become the norm again, or that this will be the normal way of things in the future. With more certainty, it is easier to predict that flexibility of working life and style will not retreat and the changes that we are experiencing now will have some long-lasting repercussions.

Whether you are a lone in-house counsel, part of a team or a team leader, it is important to recognise that compliance processes and procedures cannot be allowed to become less relevant. Compliance is often described as a dynamic process. Policies and similar which are not regularly reviewed have the unfortunate habit of becoming stale and not fit for purpose, and this creates problems when needing to prove to the SRA that it is right to have confidence in us.

Table 12 includes some thoughts about the impact that changes triggered by the pandemic may have on compliance with some suggestions as to how to demonstrate an appropriate response.

Table 12: Compliance challenges and solutions

Compliance challenge	Solution
The need for effective governance	Ensure reporting lines still work
Effective supervision	Adapt the supervision policy so that there are substitutes for the face-to-face and office-based ways of supervising colleagues Consider the new risk hotspots – the senior colleagues who are happy to work away from the team and the less experienced colleagues who continue to need appropriate mentoring
Record-keeping	Ensure that in-house solicitors are reminded of their reporting and notification duties, plus their duty to record certain breaches and other issues Have an online mechanism for the filing of reports

continued on next page

Compliance challenge	Solution
Training	Training must continue and records must be kept Ensure that there is access to online and other training resources Remind colleagues of the need to maintain accurate training records
Confidentiality issues	Update the confidentiality policy and related documentation to accommodate off-site risks Send reminders about the expectations when dealing with client matters by phone and when using computers Consider destruction policies
Case management	Now more than ever, the file history must be a complete record of instructions, conversations, decisions etc. Remind colleagues of the need for evidence to be able to justify all file actions

Key questions

- Have we spoken with the business about their expectations?
- Are these realistic expectations?
- What messages are we communicating to team members (where applicable) about the support which is offered?
- Are the correct people delivering key messages about the standards which we will continue to meet and how this will happen?
- Do we still feel like the brand ambassadors for the business?
- Do we recognise that not everyone has adapted comfortably to this way of working?
- What support is available?
- Are the right people within the team, and in the wider business, visible and accessible?
- Are we being clear about the essential compliance actions that are non-negotiable despite these changing circumstances?
- What do we consider to be the new business as usual in terms of providing legal services?

Chapter XIV: Conclusion

Regulation interest, being able to demonstrate compliance in practice and having a fundamental ethical core are all attributes which must remain constant for in-house counsel.

To help consolidate and reinforce these points, and the information contained in the previous chapters, here are some concluding thoughts contributed by another subject expert.

THOUGHT LEADERSHIP

Mandy Hargun *is a practising solicitor who has worked both in private practice and in an in-house counsel role. She now provides* *compliance and data protection-related services to other members of the profession. In this contribution, she shares some of her thoughts on the in-house practice and answers some questions based on her personal experiences.*

I worked in private practice for over 14 years until my first role as an in-house lawyer. I used to think dealing with clients was easier when in private practice, but soon came to the realisation my clients were all around me when I began working at a global corporate company. I began to have a new-found respect for the stresses that in-house lawyers encounter. I couldn't just put the phone down to my client and deal with it tomorrow; there was no tomorrow. I faced my clients on a daily basis – in the cafeteria, on the way to the toilet or in the kitchen. You can quite quickly forget when in-house, the ethics and standards of the SRA. It is important to be constantly reminded of these, and perhaps as in-house counsel, there is less information or assistance out there that can guide us. I would spend at least three days in a row on back-to-back calls with people from different time zones. It's difficult, because at times you want to talk things over with someone but being part of a small legal department that is already stretched can prove to be difficult. I often spoke to my law firm friend to run through matters to check what I was saying was accurate or whether I was just completely off track.

I suppose what I am trying to say is, that whilst an in-house counsel shouldn't be treated the same as an employee, remaining independent tends to be quite difficult and the lines often can become blurred. I quite quickly realised that it was all very well answering questions for my client, but I needed to also consider the needs of the company from an economic sense, without forgetting my ethics and integrity.

Thus, employees are fully aware that we are independent from them, forming a 'them' and 'us' barrier from the start. They aren't usually fully sure of the reason why but know that there are ethical lines that they shouldn't cross. Many times, I sensed that they felt I could not be trusted with all of the information and probed constantly for context for what was asked of me and had to dig deeper. This was just one example where perhaps your employees feel that you are bound by a different rule of ethics. Many in-house lawyers can become so entangled in considering just the economic needs of the company that the other employees too forget that we are bound by the rule of law, thus making us one of them.

- -

Q: Why can't a solicitor who is employed in-house be treated in the same way as other employees in the business?

A. In-house lawyers are in the firing line in ensuring that the company addresses matters, legally and professionally. It's important for the company and the lawyer that ethics are at the forefront of the lawyer's mind when providing advice, as failing to do so can have negative implications for the lawyer as well as the company.

Having worked in private practice for 14 years before moving in-house, there was no forgetting that I was an officer of the court and accountable for my compliance with the SRA Code of Conduct and my wider reporting obligations. If something goes wrong, the HR department or company insurance is not going to protect me as it may for a regular employee.

There is always loyalty towards the employer, which is understandable. However, the SRA imposes the standard of ethics and integrity and competence that is expected from in-house lawyers. Failing to meet these standards would result in an invitation for regulatory action by the SRA. Whilst often in-house lawyers have to consider advising the company and considering their obligations of compliance, the economic pressures of a company cannot outweigh accountability for compliance with the SRA Code of Conduct.

So, whilst you and your regular employees may enjoy the same benefits and be on the same payroll, there is a need to maintain a certain independence from the company by compliance to the Code. This in turn can uphold public confidence by assimilating ethics and rule of law into the company.

Q. What conversations does a solicitor need to have with their employer so that the employer understands their regulated position?

A. I think it is important that the employer is aware that in-house lawyers must adhere to the SRA Code of Conduct and all other applicable rules where they oversee lawyers in different jurisdictions. Employers should note that lawyers have an obligation to report matters that may either amount to a breach of regulatory requirements or that need investigating, whether a breach has occurred, by any person and not just the lawyer. At times, you have to play the 'bad guy' by pushing back on certain matters where the loyalties to your employer are overridden by the public interest. As an in-house lawyer, you're an important stakeholder in the business and there are very few decisions that are taken without your advice or knowledge, so it's important for the employer to understand that your professional ethics will not be compromised and that you have a duty to report and not just turn a blind eye.

Q. How does an in-house solicitor demonstrate compliance with SRA requirements?

A. The Code for Solicitors requires us to justify our decisions and actions in order to demonstrate compliance with our obligations under the SRA's regulatory arrangements (Rule 7.2). Quite often, in-house lawyers take calls back-to-back, offering advice to different departments. One way to demonstrate compliance would be to introduce systems and controls. Companies have internal policies and local SOPs; this can assist in demonstrating compliance in main areas, such as conflict. Then, to have a system to ensure written justification of the decision making when not following these policies.

"As an in-house lawyer, you're an important stakeholder in the business and there are very few decisions that are taken without your advice or knowledge."

It is easy to misconstrue or misunderstand the advice given. This is the reason why in-house lawyers should always write it down. I always sent an email at the end of each day confirming the advice given. At times, this is not always possible as you are constantly on the go, but I always tried to write down advice given to higher-level management where you're more likely to deal with ethical questions.

- -

Q. What knowledge and skills does an in-house solicitor need which might be different from the needs of private practitioners?

A. *Commercial awareness* – as with any business, it is important to understand how the business works and the products and services it offers. This can take many months, especially when you work in a global business. As a key stakeholder, you get pulled into many projects and decision-making processes, not all of which may necessarily require legal advice, so it's important to have a business-like attitude when approaching decisions. It is important to work with the business to come up with legally sound solutions, which in turn does not amount to profit loss.

Broad legal knowledge – there are many departments in a business; you could be asked to advise on many aspects of law, and whilst there is assistance from external counsel, you should be able to provide broad advice to the business.

Speaking to colleagues – in private practice, you are constantly speaking to other lawyers, and you can use legal jargon. However, in-house lawyers need to ensure that they are able to communicate with the business at different levels. Not everyone understands legal or technical words or the nature or importance of the advice you are giving; simplicity is key. You also should be able to train your employees so that they are able to do their jobs ethically and with compliance.

Managing outside counsel – in-house lawyers almost always have access to a law firm they use for advice in areas where in-house counsel does not specialise.

Good project management skills – you will be juggling different projects at different times. In practice, you tend to only manage your own case load and can shift deadlines. However, when in-house, other departments will be waiting on your deliverables and will generally have a road map for completion which coincides with wider interests which cannot be delayed, such as launches on products that are date specific and have been heavily advertised to the public.

- -

Q. What tips would you give an in-house solicitor?

A. • *Get to know the business and your colleagues.* Often, in-house lawyers in global companies jet-set around the world, getting to personally know middle- and higher-level management as they would usually be the ones coming to the lawyer for advice. It's also important to go to manufacturing bases to understand what the company does and their ethos.

- • *Be bold and confident!* You need to be able to stand by your decisions and say no where you need to.

- • *Know your role, especially if you wear more than one hat.* Quite often in-house lawyers are directors or vice presidents, and conflicting roles can be difficult to manage but remember your professional and ethical obligation to your regulator.

- • *Don't compromise your integrity.*

- • *Read things twice if you have to before signing off.*

- • *Avoid legal jargon.* Unlike in practice, you are conversing with non-lawyers, so using simple language is key to good understanding and communication.

- • *Try to find solutions with your client rather than saying no from the outset.*

- • *Manage your projects and your inbox!* It's a fast-paced environment with projects delayed or expedited all the time.

- • *Implement systems and controls and train your colleagues on how to follow them.*

About the author

Tracey Calvert
Director, Oakalls Consultancy Limited
tcalvert@oakallsconsultancy.co.uk

Tracey Calvert is a lawyer and the director of Oakalls Consultancy Limited. She is a regulatory, compliance and ethics specialist providing a variety of advisory services to members of the solicitor's profession.

Tracey is a regular speaker and trainer on these topics and has delivered presentations both within the UK and internationally. She is the co-chair of the International Bar Association's Professional Ethics Committee and is on the editorial board of the Law Society's Legal Compliance Bulletin. She is a contributor to *Cordery on Legal Services*, writes a monthly compliance column for the *Solicitors Journal* and has written several books on compliance and ethics. Full details are available at www.oakallsconsultancy.co.uk.

Tracey was previously employed by the Law Society and the SRA as a senior ethics adviser and a policy executive. She has also worked both in private practice and in an in-house role.

Index

About Globe Law and Business

Globe Law and Business was established in 2005. From the very beginning, we set out to create law books which are sufficiently high level to be of real use to the experienced professional, yet still accessible and easy to navigate. Most of our authors are drawn from Magic Circle and other top commercial firms, both in the UK and internationally.

Our titles are carefully produced, with the utmost attention paid to editorial, design and production processes. We hope this results in high-quality publications that are easy to read, and a pleasure to own. Our titles are also available as ebooks, which are compatible with most desktop, laptop and tablet devices. In 2018 we expanded our portfolio to include journals and Special Reports, available both digitally and in hard copy format, and produced to the same high standards as our books.

In the Spring of 2021, we were very pleased to announce the start of a new chapter for Globe Law and Business following the acquisition of law books under the imprint Ark Publishing. We are very much looking forward to working with our new Ark authors, many of whom are well-known to us, and to further developing the law firm management list, among other areas.

We'd very much like to hear from you with your thoughts and ideas for improving what we offer. Please do feel free to email me at sian@globelawandbusiness.com with your views.

Sian O'Neill
Managing director
Globe Law and Business
www.globelawandbusiness.com